Computers in Knowledge-Based Fields

A Joint Project of
The Industrial Relations Section
Sloan School of Management
Massachusetts Institute of Technology and
The Inter-University Study of Labor Problems in Economic Development

Computers in Knowledge-Based Fields

Charles A. Myers

The MIT Press   Cambridge, Massachusetts, and London, England

Preface

This study is the last of the series of research projects on the implications of technological change and automation, undertaken by the Industrial Relations Section of the Sloan School of Management at M.I.T. A number of earlier publications (as noted in the Introduction) have emerged from this effort, which has had general support from a five-year Ford Foundation grant to the Sloan School. This has been supplemented by other funds from the International Business Machines Corporation and the Manpower Administration of the U.S. Department of Labor.

The research and released time for this particular study were also supported in part by funds from the Inter-University Study of Labor Problems in Economic Development in which I have been associated with Clark Kerr, John T. Dunlop, and Frederick Harbison since 1952. I appreciate the suggestions of some of my colleagues in the Sloan School who have taken the time to read sections of earlier drafts of this monograph in "working paper" form: Professors John F. Rockart, G. Anthony Gorry, Douglass V. Brown, and Dr. William Kennedy. The section on libraries benefited from the comments of Professor William N. Locke, Director of the M.I.T. Libraries; Miss Natalie N. Nicholson, Associate Director; and Professor J. Francis Reintjes, Director of the Engineering Systems Laboratory, which is working on a Project INTREX prototype. Robert P. Bigelow, Esq., of Boston was helpful in reviewing the chapter dealing with legal and legislative services; he is one of the pioneers in the application of computers in these fields.

I am greatly indebted to my former graduate research assistant, Ephraim R. McLean 3rd, now Assistant Professor of Management at the University of California at Los Angeles. During 1967–1968 he collected materials from a variety of sources, conducted some interviews, and reported on several meetings and conferences. Subsequently, he was helpful with later references and made detailed comments on the first draft of the entire manuscript.

This monograph could not have been completed, however, without the help of my secretary, Patricia Macpherson, who typed more drafts than I care to mention, checked references, and handled other problems connected with the research and writing over at least two years, without neglecting her other responsibilities.

Charles A. Myers

Cambridge, Massachusetts
March 1970

Introduction

In less than two decades, the number of computers in use in the United States has increased from around 100 in 1955 to close to 60,000 today, with many more on order by expectant users.[1] The power and capabilities of modern computers, furthermore, are far greater than the "first generation" machines used in the initial applications. While the computer revolution has been spreading around the world, particularly in Western Europe, Japan, and the Soviet bloc, the use of computers in the United States is far in advance of most countries.[2] Thus, our experience may be a forecast of future applications in other world areas. This is particularly true for the less developed countries that tend to borrow modern technology from advanced countries, in this case with the assistance of U.S. computer manufacturers.

Perhaps the major impact of computers in the United States, as well as in other technologically advanced countries, is in the management of organizations. The literature on this experience is voluminous and growing. Even recent evaluations tend to get out of date, as improved technology ("hardware") and associated programs ("software"), along with management science techniques, are improved and gain broader acceptance by management.

Nevertheless, it is useful to stand apart from the specific applications and raise questions about the broader implications of computers on organization structures, the nature of work, the resistance to change, and the means of

[1]Estimates obviously vary. The figures cited were used by the Bureau of Labor Statistics in 1967, and 80,000 computers were forecast for 1975. But a different estimate has been used by Edward J. Brenner, U.S. Commissioner of Patents: 60,000 by 1970 and 85,000 by 1975. "Computer Software Unpatentable," *The New York Times,* October 23, 1968, p. 59. A later IBM advertisement stated: "Fifteen years ago there were a handful of computers. Today there are more than 60,000 in use. And today's most advanced computers are about 1,000 times faster and process information about 100 times cheaper than the one (IBM delivered) in 1953." *The New York Times,* December 29, 1968.

[2]An estimate as of December 1967 put U.S. "computer power" at 39,500, West Germany (3,500), Japan (3,000), Britain (2,800), France (2,200), U.S.S.R. (1,750), and China (mainland—2,530). These are clearly rough data. *Newsweek,* vol. 2, no. 5, January 29, 1968, p. 57.

gaining acceptance of the new technology. This was the objective of an earlier research effort in the Industrial Relations Section of the Sloan School of Management,[3] and of subsequent studies and research conferences to assess the impact of computers on job-man matching systems[4] and on collective bargaining.[5] These questions were also explored in a special study of the effect of computers and other technological systems on the attitudes of office workers toward their jobs.[6]

The present study is an assessment of the experience with computer applications in some knowledge-based fields, exclusive of those already mentioned. Obviously, there are many knowledge-based areas in which computers are useful,[7] but this study will cover only the following major fields:

1. Formal education, including the administration of educational institutions.

2. Library systems and subsystems.

[3]Charles A. Myers (ed.), *The Impact of Computers on Management,* Cambridge, Mass.: M.I.T. Press, 1967, and Myers, "The Impact of EDP on Management Organization and Managerial Work," Working Paper 139-65, Sloan School of Management, M.I.T., September 1965. This work was supported by a grant to the Sloan School from the Ford Foundation, and the research conference had a supplementary grant from the International Business Machines Corporation.

[4]Frazier Kellogg, *Computer-Based Job Matching Systems,* multilithed summary proceedings and report of a conference held at M.I.T. in January 1967. The conference was funded by a grant from the Manpower Administration, U.S. Department of Labor, and the research was supported from the grant by the Ford Foundation to the Sloan School of Management. A subsequent monograph by Frazier Kellogg, *Computer-Based Aids to the Placement Process,* was published by the Industrial Relations Section, Sloan School of Management, M.I.T., in February 1969.

[5]Abraham J. Siegel (ed.), *The Impact of Computers on Collective Bargaining,* Cambridge, Mass.: The M.I.T. Press, 1969. This book grew out of papers and discussion at a research conference held at M.I.T. in April 1968, supported by a grant from the Ford Foundation to the Sloan School of Management.

[6]Jon M. Shepard, *Automation and Alienation: A Study of Office and Factory Workers* (in press), 1970. This study of office jobs in five insurance companies and a large bank, testing hypotheses growing out of the author's earlier study in manufacturing, was financed from the Ford Foundation grant and a supplementary grant from the Manpower Administration of the U.S. Department of Labor.

[7]See Fritz Machlup, *The Production and Distribution of Knowledge in the United States,* Princeton, N.J.: Princeton University Press, 1962. Machlup includes as part of "education" the mother's education of children in the

3. Legal and legislative services; administration of justice; crime prevention and law enforcement.

4. Medical and hospital services.

5. National and centralized local data banks for research and administrative uses.

The omissions from this list will be apparent to the reader. Nonacademic training methods that rely on computer-aided instruction (CAI) are similar to CAI in formal education. Consequently, they are omitted to avoid duplication. Research in science, engineering, social sciences, and even in humanities, which has benefited from the computational prowess of digital computers as well as from their capacity to permit rapid simulations, is not included simply because the task of reviewing this "experience" is too great. Clearly, advanced econometric techniques used in economic forecasting, such as the Brookings model or the University of Pennsylvania model, would have been impossible without digital computers. Many other examples could be cited; but "research" as such is not included in the analysis since it takes place in many different private and governmental organizations— not merely in formal educational institutions.

Even in the five fields that are the subject of this study, it is impossible to cover all of the recent developments. Computer· applications are moving rapidly in each of these, and no report can be complete or up-to-date. Indeed, a general cutoff point was adopted for the extensive period of data collection and bibliographic search: January 1, 1969. Subsequent review of the first draft of the manuscript by a number of colleagues led to additional later information,

---

home, church schools, on-the-job training, education in the armed services, and libraries. But even this broad definition of education fails to encompass all of the knowledge industry, in Machlup's definition. Research and development, printing and publishing, broadcasting, movies and the theater, information machinery, professional services, and telephone and telegraph were part of the "production and distribution of knowledge." All of this totaled $136 billion, or almost 30 percent of the GNP in 1958. For a later updating of Machlup's figures, see Gilbert Burck, "Knowledge: The Biggest Growth Industry of Them All," *Fortune,* vol. LXX, no. 5, November 1964, pp. 128–131ff. This article claimed that "the knowledge industry" had a 43 percent growth in the preceding five years.

and at various points important new developments have been included. But no claim is made for complete coverage of recent developments.

In the chapters to follow, each dealing with one of the five knowledge-based areas listed earlier, the information and analysis are intended to provide some answers to the following main themes or questions:

1. What are the *needs* that encouraged or required the use of computers?

2. What were the principal *initial* or early applications of computers, and what problems did they encounter?

3. What have been *some* of the more *recent* efforts to utilize computers, and how have they differed in their objectives and results? Can anything be said about comparative costs of computer-based programs as compared with other programs?

4. What are the *implications* of computers for the nature of the work performed, and the ways in which it is organized or is likely to be organized in the future? What is the evolving nature of the man-machine relationship?

5. What have been the *resistances* to computer introductions? How have people reacted to them, and what has been the experience in getting people to accept new ways of working with computer-based systems?

The more important questions, to which the others provide necessary background, are the last two. In each field, it is essential to try to understand what the implications of computers are for the nature of jobs, the organization of work, the people affected, and what all of this means for further developments in computer applications. In this analysis, it is also important to distinguish between the present and near-term future as distinguished from longer-run possibilities.

In other words, what is the "reality" and what is the "vision" in computer impacts on these knowledge-based fields? It is as important to look at this difference, as it is for any student of computers to be specific about his time horizons. One specialist concerned with the impact of computers on education has indicated the difference which this time horizon can make:

I am manic-depressive about the future of educational technology: manic about the long-term possibilities which are extraordinary, and depressive about the short-run. No significant changes in the American education system during the next decade will be the direct result of current experiments with computers in education. It will take twenty or thirty years to overcome the social, economic, and technical factors that are retarding the use of computers in education.[8]

This perceptive comment indicates the possibility that many of the initial and even recent developments in computer applications may have been oversold by enthusiasts, who underestimate the factors that widen the gap between limited, experimental use of computers in knowledge-based areas and widespread adoption of computer-based systems. Even if the technological problems (both hardware and software) are solved, there remain economic constraints and human or social resistances. Quite apart from the latter, man always has a *comparative* economic advantage over a computer that technologically might eventually be able to replicate man's intelligence. This indicates the prospect of *man-machine* systems for the indefinite future.[9]

In the following chapters, we shall examine in more detail the nature of these constraints and the probability of evolutionary rather than revolutionary change as computers are used more extensively in these knowledge-based areas.

[8]Professor Anthony G. Oettinger of Harvard University, speaking at the opening M.I.T. Colloquium on Computers and Education, Spring Term 1968, as reported in *The Technology Review,* vol. 70, no. 6, April 1968, p. 50. See also Anthony G. Oettinger, with the collaboration of Sema Marks, *Run, Computer, Run: The Mythology of Educational Innovation,* Cambridge, Mass.: Harvard University Press, 1969. This book grew out of several of Oettinger's earlier articles and papers, including some referred to later in this monograph.

[9]Herbert A. Simon, *The New Science of Management Decisions,* New York: Harper & Row, Publishers, 1960, pp. 33–34. For a similar view by another pioneer in the long-run implications of information technology, see Thomas L. Whisler, *Information Technology and Organizational Change,* Belmont Calif.: Wadsworth Publishing Company, 1970, especially Chapter 7, "The Long Run—Prospects and Problems."

1. Formal Education and Educational Administration

Education is clearly the leading knowledge-based industry.[1] Student enrollments have expanded at all levels each year, and investment in educational plant and equipment is mounting. But, for the most part, education has not been capital intensive in the usual sense; expenditures are primarily on salaries and services, real estate, buildings, furniture, and books. Some technological aids have been used, primarily audiovisual aids and programmed instruction, as in language laboratories. But when the Subcommittee on Economic Progress of the Joint Economic Committee considered the implications of computer-aided instruction (CAI), it concluded:

The prospective increased use of expensive communication equipment and systems involves much greater capital investment in equipment, and the employment of technicians to install and maintain it. This is a new phenomenon in the field of education. Educators who think primarily in terms of operating costs for classroom teaching will be required to change their accounting notions to accommodate certain fixed costs for instructional equipment to be amortized over time.[2]

While the future possibilities of technological breakthroughs in education are unlimited, principally through CAI, the present reality is quite different. The sharp contrast between the short-run and the long-run (20 to 30 years) was succinctly expressed last year by Professor Anthony Oettinger of Harvard in the statement quoted in the introduction to this book.[3] Others agree with his diagnosis:

[1] Clark Kerr put it this way: "The American economy was built around railroads in the last half of the 19th century, around the automobile in the first two-thirds of this century, and it will be built around education in the balance of this century." Quoted in *Report of the Subcommittee on Economic Progress of the Joint Economic Committee of the Congress,* Washington, D.C.: August 1966, p. 7.

[2] *Ibid.,* p. 8.

[3] Quoted in *The Technology Review,* vol. 70, no. 6, April 1968, p. 50. However, "Oettinger's pessimistic conclusions....were disputed by a number of conference participants," Wayne H. Holtzman, "Conference on Computer-Assisted Instruction, Testing, and Guidance," University of Texas, October 21–22, 1968, *Items,* vol. 22, no. 4, December 1968, Social Science Research Council, New York, pp. 43–48. For a restatement of Oettinger's views, and replies by some of his critics, see Anthony Oettinger and Sema Marks, "Educational Technology: New Myths and Old

Although computer-aided instruction has served well as a research and demonstration tool, it is still in its infancy. It has not yet become a practical instructional tool ready for widespread implementation in public schools; indeed most of the problems must be solved prior to its widespread application have yet to be solved. However, the rate of development of on-line computer usage for individualized instruction is very rapid and deserves serious attention by school planners.[4]

There is little evidence to show that the computer will find a substantial market as a teaching machine for at least five years, and more likely for 10 or 15. Much research remains to be done. Projections through 1970 for the market for "electronic and related equipment" in all schools is $7.5 million, as compared with $5.5 million in 1965. Computer-aided instruction is estimated at less than 6 percent of the total 1970 market for tape recorders, language labs, movie projectors, overhead projectors, standard TV and closed-circuit TV receivers—totalling $113.5 million in 1970.[5]

But some disagree with these views. While a majority of those attending an "instructional systems seminar" in August 1967 insisted that "CAI is just for research now," a smaller group viewed "CAI as an instrument for teaching *now* — to supplement, or compliment, if not to replace, conventional classroom instruction."[6]

Realities," *Harvard Educational Review,* vol. 38, no. 4, Fall 1968, pp. 697–755 (also Reprint Number 6, Harvard University Program on Science and Technology). For a fuller expansion of these views, see Oettinger, *Run, Computer, Run,* Cambridge, Mass.: Harvard University Press, 1969, especially Chaps. 5 and 6.

[4] Harry F. Silberman, Systems Development Corporation, Santa Monica, California, in unpublished paper, "Applications of Computers in Education," presented at the American Management Association Conference on Education and Training, New York, August 8, 1967.

[5] Dwight C. Macauley, "The Market Outlook for Instructional Technology," Arthur D. Little, Inc., Cambridge, Mass., October 1966, p. 16 and data in Table 7, p. 14. This view is supported by a prediction that by 1978 "the majority of schools will have independent study facilities equipped with audio and visual components," but only "about 25 per cent of the schools will have on-line use of computers for instructional purposes—drill, tutorial, simulation, problem solving and information retrieval." Robert W. Locke and David Engler, "Run, Strawman, Run: A Critique of Dr. Anthony G. Oettinger's Essay on Educational Technology, Run, Computer, Run," McGraw-Hill Book Company, New York, April 1968 (mimeographed) p. 22.

[6] Robert M. Gordon, summarizing results of seminar sponsored by the Science Research Associates, a subsidiary of IBM, in Chicago, August 2–4, 1967, *Datamation,* vol. 13, no. 9, September 1967, p. 70.

These views are best evaluated after a brief review of current experience with computer-aided instruction and other computer applications in education. The remainder of this chapter will consider the needs to be met, first steps and principal recent applications in the administration of educational services (in primary, secondary, and higher education), estimates of costs, implications of CAI for people and organizations, and resistances to be encountered. A summary of technical and nontechnical problems in computer applications in education will conclude the chapter.

The Needs

Faced with a shortage of teachers as enrollments expand, educational institutions may find that computers will assist instruction and administration in meeting the following needs:

1. To relieve teachers of repetitive, structured, drill-type work, as in elementary and some secondary mathematics, reading, spelling, and grading routine exercises. These are the tasks that are often unattractive to teachers. It is also possible that CAI will help students to *understand* rather than learn by rote, memorizing without understanding.

2. To provide teachers with continuous evaluation of their student's work, in a system that stores records of student performance on assignments, drills, and examinations, and then gives the teacher a periodic cumulative printout.

3. To permit slower students to set their own pace in CAI, thus avoiding peer group and teacher pressure. One report indicated that "poorer students reacted best to CAI. They felt they were receiving more attention and were less conscious of peer pressure."[7] This is the need for more *individualized* instruction, as is the next point.

4. To permit faster or advanced students to use the

[7] Mrs. Sylvia Charp, Director of Instructional Systems, Philadelphia School District, in discussion at American Management Association Conference on Education and Training, New York, August 9, 1967. The same claim has been made by the Stanford program, discussed in the next section.

computer for more difficult work, or "as a facile and literalistic slave which they can learn from by ordering him around" (to use a phrase from the M.I.T. Colloquium on Computers and Education). The emphasis here would be on computer-aided *learning* rather than on instruction as such, and would involve learning to write programs and to interact with the computer in an on-line real-time sense.[8] This would permit students to enlarge their educational experience, by enabling them to simulate environments not normally accessible or to explore complex or abstract concepts.

5. To improve instruction in basic structured subjects, which are not being taught effectively in many schools and colleges because of large enrollments and teacher shortages. Such subjects might include some parts of geometry, biology, basic psychology, foreign languages, library science, and others.

6. To assist educational administrators in the complex and time-consuming tasks of classroom and course scheduling, preparation of student programs, keeping of student records, preparing payrolls, provisional budgets, and other financial records. In a more sophisticated sense, computer-aided systems analysis could aid administrators in allocating more effectively the total resources (financial, physical, and human) available for a given period.

7. An additional need, not related to the pressure on enrollments or the teacher shortage, is for students to understand and work with computers themselves. Computer systems will increasingly become a part of people's lives, and the opportunity for students at all educational levels to get "hands on" use of computers, to understand their benefits as well as their limitations, is still too limited. A broader understanding of how computers work is a pressing educational need.

---

[8] These points were stressed during the weekly Colloquium on Computers and Education sponsored at M.I.T. by the staff of the Education Research Center. The emphasis on computer-aided learning was also made at the colloquium by Professor Ralph W. Gerard, University of California (Irvine), May 1, 1968.

Some Initial Steps

Initial developments in computer-aided instruction have been influenced by the earlier experience with noncomputerized "programmed instruction," including the "teaching machines" that were introduced between 1955 and 1960. The initial interest in the latter apparently soured. As one study observed, "What the teaching machine fiasco really proved is that no machine can be designed to impart knowledge until the builder of the machine understands the learning and teaching process."[9] Some programmed instruction utilized frames on teaching machines; some involved programmed texts. A review of this experience in 1962 for the Fund for the Advancement of Education concluded:

Although the research gives us little reason to be satisfied with the theories and the standards of today's programming, and every reason to believe that it will be possible some day to make programs vastly more effective than today's programs, nevertheless programmed instruction shows signs of hardening, partly under commercial pressure, into a fixed and mechanical technology, with theories and procedures taken for granted.[10]

While the chronological sequence of early computer-aided instruction programs is difficult to determine, there were at least two such efforts in 1964. A computer-based "laboratory for Learning and Teaching" was established at Stanford University in 1964, under the direction of Professor Patrick Suppes. It has subsequently received considerable publicity for the variety of CAI programs it has developed and tested at the primary, secondary, and even college level. (These will be noted in the next section.)

Another pioneer effort was apparently the "Talking

[9] Macauley, "The Market Outlook for Instructional Technology," p. 6.

[10] Wilbur Schramm, *Programmed Instruction—Today and Tomorrow,* New York: The Fund for the Advancement of Education, 1962, p. ii. Subsequently, Schramm edited *Four Case Studies of Programmed Instruction* for the Fund published in 1964, and concluded, "On the basis of these studies, it appears that truly individualized instruction with programmed material can be achieved only by a really major change in the context of teaching and learning." P. 15.

Typewriter," growing out of an early development by Professor O. K. Moore, formerly of Yale and now at Ohio State University. It has been used in teaching reading and writing, especially for disadvantaged children in the Brownsville Section of Brooklyn, and with kindergarten and beginning primary grades in various cities.[11]

Some Recent Applications

These are best reviewed in terms of primary, secondary, and higher education.

Primary Education

1. The Stanford group, now known as the Institute for Mathematical Studies in the Social Sciences, has developed computer-based mathematics instruction for both (a) individualized drill and practice, for grades 1 through 6, in cities in California, Mississippi, Kentucky, and Iowa, and (b) tutorial systems in which the student is given basic concepts and skills, at his own pace. In the latter, the computer program has the main responsibility. In contrast, the drill and practice system "is designed to supplement what the teacher does in the classroom. So we're restricted to what the teacher does, not what we think she should do. No curriculum design is involved at this stage."[12] An evaluation of these programs through May 1969 indicates that drill and practice mathematics programs in Mississippi showed positive results from grades 1 to 6 and some in California in comparison with matched control groups. The tutorial math program run for culturally deprived students

---

[11] Information supplied by the Responsive Environments Corporation, which markets the McGraw-Edison computerized "Talking Typewriter."

[12] Patrick Suppes, "The Teacher and Computer-Assisted Instruction," *NEA Journal,* vol. 56, no. 2, February 1967, pp. 15–17. In the fall of 1968, the drill and practice program was used by 2,000 children, and the tutorial systems were in use by first-graders in one California school and by fourth-graders in another. Suppes has characterized the former as "a strict operational implementation of individualized drill-and-practice in elementary mathematics." During 1968–1969 the number of students involved was over 7,000. Patrick Suppes, reply to Oettinger and Marks, *Harvard Educational Review,* vol. 38, no. 4, Fall 1968, p. 37. For a full report on the Stanford program, see Patrick Suppes and Mona Morningstar, "Evaluation of Three Computer-Assisted Instructional Programs," Technical Report No. 142, May 2, 1969, Institute for Mathematical Studies in the Social Sciences, Stanford University, Stanford, Calif.

in California had a significant positive effect for slow learners in the first grade.

The Stanford group is also apparently working toward "dialogue systems," but these remain some distance away, "because a number of technical problems remain unsolved. One problem is the difficulty of devising a computer that can 'understand' oral communication, especially of young children."[13] The research has been supported by grants from the National Science Foundation and the U.S. Office of Education.

2. A computerized program for teaching elementary mathematics (really addition and subtraction) and spelling is being tried in 16 public schools in New York City.[14]

3. Bolt Beranek & Newman Inc. (a Cambridge, Massachusetts, technical consulting firm) has developed a new computer language (LOGO) to "stamp out fuzzy thinking and teach third grade mathematics in some suburban schools."[15]

Secondary Education

1. Several efforts have been made in high schools to teach computer programming to students. One for junior high school students in Santa Monica, California, was developed, but apparently the first course on computer mathematics in any high school was started in a New York City high school early in 1964.[16]

2. An experimental CAI program for elementary mathematics in Massachusetts also involves encouraging students to "teach the computer by writing their own programs." This has been developed by the Massachusetts State Department of Education for grades 9 to 11 in several suburban schools. In a normal classroom, "a student would not have a chance to teach someone else.

[13] Suppes, *NEA Journal*, p. 16.

[14] *The New York Times*, March 19, 1968. The Stanford computer was used for this application until RCA installed one in New York City.

[15] As reported by two staff members at the M.I.T. Colloquium, Spring 1968.

[16] As reported in *The New York Times*, April 16, 1964. For the Santa Monica experience, see Silberman, unpublished paper, "Applications of Computers in Education," p. 3.

The project has turned into one to determine how to get kids and computers together" rather than using the computer for drill and practice only.[17]

3. The School of Education at the University of Illinois has been developing a computer-based system known as "Plato" over a number of years, using it first for the instruction of maternity nurses and later for some secondary school subjects, particularly algebra, geometry, and foreign languages. The system will ultimately involve some 4,000 student terminals, each with a key-set and a plasma-display device that is expected to be substantially cheaper than the usual cathode-ray tube. The terminals and displays are tied to a central computer, but the displays also permit projection of locally stored information.[18]

Higher Education

The expanding use of computers in colleges and universities means that more and more students are learning to use computers as part of their formal courses as well as in research projects. In 1967, an official of the National Science Foundation reported that approximately two-thirds of all college students were attending colleges and universities with computer facilities of some sort, and this proportion is undoubtedly rising each year.[19] Few of tomorrow's college graduates will be computer ignoramuses, as many of yesterday's still are.

1. Dartmouth College students learn a simplified English-like language called BASIC, developed by Professor John

[17] As reported by Dr. Jesse O. Richardson, Massachusetts State Department of Education, Colloquium Series on Computers and Education, sponsored by the Education Research Center of M.I.T., February 28, 1968.

[18] Donald L. Bitzer at M.I.T. Colloquium Series, February 14, 1968; and also as reported by Wayne H. Holtzman, *Items,* p. 44. Criticisms of this system are reported in the latter reference.

[19] The need for expanding computer facilities to all colleges and universities was stressed by the Report of the President's Science Advisory Committee, *Computers in Higher Education,* The White House, Washington, D.C.: February 1967 (known as the Pierce Report, after the Chairman of the Panel on Computers in Higher Education). The Panel estimated that a 4 percent increase ($60 per student per year) in higher education budgets would be necessary by 1971–1972, and recommended that the federal government provide three-fourths of this increase.

Kemeny, Chairman of the Mathematics Department (now president of Dartmouth). This language is implemented on a large GE time-sharing computer system. Professor Kemeny claims that about 80 percent of the students are proficient BASIC programmers, with the business school students being the largest users. By early 1969 the Dartmouth program involved participation by 16 other colleges and 22 secondary schools, mostly in New Hampshire, through leased wires to the central computer. According to Kemeny, the greatest learning experience for the student is in teaching the computer how to do something, because "if you really want to learn something, teach it to someone else."[20]

2. Civil Engineering students at M.I.T. use a computer in the department for solving design problems. Other M.I.T. students have used separate computers (as in the Sloan Building for Economics and Management), but the move is toward terminals tied in to the central M.I.T. Computation Center or to Project MAC (Machine-Aided Cognition or Multiple Access Computer), which was the prototype of all time-sharing systems.

3. An effort has been made in the Sloan School of Management at M.I.T. to develop an "associative learning instructional system" as part of the first-year graduate course in management information and control systems (management accounting).[21] While still an experimental prototype, the system is intended to offer the student an "associative memory" to related concepts and fields as it provides him with interactive flexible search procedures and has the ability to learn and adapt on the basis of his progress. In other words, this goes beyond systems that have only matching of programmed responses.

4. The Stanford University Institute for Mathematical Studies in the Social Sciences began experimenting late in

[20] At the M.I.T. Colloquium on Education and Computers, April 17, 1968.

[21] Zenon S. Zannetos and Michael Scott Morton, *Efforts Toward an Associative Learning Instructional System*, Sloan School of Management, M.I.T., Working Paper 355-68, August 1968. This work is continuing under a three-year grant from the Ford Foundation.

1957 with completely computerized first-year and second-year Russian language courses, programmed by a professor of Slavic Languages at Stanford. This purports to eliminate the classroom sessions completely; language laboratory and homework are in the automated program. There were fewer dropouts in the computerized sections of the first-year course during 1967–1968 than in the regular sections with a teacher in the classroom. Of 19 students enrolled in the second-year course in 1968–1969, 12 had been in the computer-based first-year class.[22] Language instruction is clearly more structured than many other college-level subjects. Professor Suppes, Director of the Institute, admits that more complex programming would be necessary for the "discussion-type" subjects, such as history, literature, and many of the social sciences. He sees CAI in these subjects as "some distance away."[23]

5. A "learner-Controlled Statistics Course" has been developed in California to permit the student to chart his own path through the course.[24] Using "maps" of the course in different degrees of detail, the student selects (with a light pen on a cathode-ray tube) those parts in which he feels he needs most help. The computer also audits his progress. This type of programming requires a much greater computer storage capacity than does a completely structured course, illustrating again the greater complexity involved. At the same time, it has a greater appeal to those students who want *less structure,* preferring to search out their own material at their own pace, as in individualized study in a library.

6. The Plato system developed at the University of

---

[22] Suppes and Morningstar, "Evaluation of Three Computer-Assisted Instructional Programs," pp. 39–42.

[23] Oral comments at M.I.T. Colloquium, March 6, 1968.

[24] Ralph E. Grubb, paper presented to American Management Association Conference, New York, August 1967. The paper was earlier reproduced by IBM, Los Gatos, California, April 5, 1967. Subsequent evaluation of this course indicates that students scored higher on posttests than did their counterparts under traditional methods. Grubb, "A Study of Differential Treatments in the Learning of Elementary Statistics" (paper presented at DAVI Conference, Portland, Oreg., April 28, 1969 - mimeographed).

Illinois (mentioned earlier) has also been used for parts of courses in electrical engineering, biology, and library science. Evaluation reports are rather general, but the program is claimed to have wide applicability.

7. First-year students in German have had up to two and one-half hours per week of practice on a computer-based system at the Stony Brook campus of the State University of New York, beginning in 1967–1968. While the CAI students were similar to other groups in speaking and understanding spoken German, they were markedly superior in reading and writing the language.[25]

8. Several universities claim to have developed CAI programs for college physics. Among these are Florida State University (which also has had a CAI course in college chemistry under development), and the Center for Research in Learning and Teaching at M.I.T., which uses a computer for mathematical models of high velocities, and for visual display of a space-time diagram that can be changed as velocity is changed by the student.

Administration of Educational Services

Among these programs are computer grading of student examinations and papers; computer-programmed student counseling and vocational guidance; class scheduling; management information systems to monitor progress toward educational objectives; and computer systems for optimum allocation of educational resources, as well as for preparing payrolls, accounting, and so on.

A few examples illustrate computer applications in these areas:

1. Computer-graded examinations are used as a part of "computer-monitored" instruction at Long Island University in New York. The University of Connecticut has experimented with a computer program for grading high school English compositions, and the reported results were found to be indistinguishable from grades assigned to the same papers by a panel of four high school and four

[25] "CAI and Language Skills," *Educational Technology,* vol. 9, no. 2, February 1969, News Notes section (no paging).

college English teachers. It is claimed that the program analyzes not only spelling, grammar, and syntax but even makes assessment for "sense."[26]

2. Student program counseling was developed in 1968 to assist the student in preparing his program for the following year, through a series of questions written into the computer program. According to the report, students preferred the nonhuman counselor, which was more responsive to student preferences than the human counselor, who tried to suggest what the student should or should not take.[27] Of course, the question of whether student preferences should always prevail is another issue.

3. A computer-based information system for vocational decisions is being developed by the Graduate School of Education at Harvard University, in collaboration with the New England Education Data Systems (NEEDS) and the Newton, Massachusetts, public school system. The program is to be so designed that a student can relate knowledge about himself to data about education, training, and work, and thereby create a body of information in which he can base his career decision. The entire program links person, computer, and teacher as counselor in such a way that the student can conduct a dialogue with the computer, while the counselor assists in interpreting and evaluating the results of the dialogue.[28] A prototype system was in operation by mid-1969.

4. The School Scheduling System has been developed at Stanford University for use by secondary schools. This computerized service provides scheduling services for a substantial number of schools throughout the United States.[29] Purdue University has developed a program that

[26] As reported by Dr. Louis Bright of the U.S. Office of Education at M.I.T. Colloquium, April 10, 1968. For a fuller account of the Connecticut experience, see Ellis B. Page (University of Connecticut), "The Use of the Computer in Analyzing Student Essays," *International Review of Education,* vol. XIV, no. 2, 1968, pp. 210–225.

[27] As reported by Harry F. Silberman, Systems Development Corporation, Santa Monica, Calif., in talk at American Management Association Conference, New York, August 9, 1968.

[28] Information Systems for Vocational Decisions, *Annual Report* (Harvard Graduate School of Education), 1966–1967, pp. 1–2. The project is financed by a grant from the U.S. Office of Education.

[29] For details, see Robert N. Bush and Donald H. Delay (both of

uses as its criteria the efficient use of classroom space, student's course preferences, and professor's preferences. Students got their own preferences 76 percent of the time, according to one report, as compared to 22 percent before. These student preferences were apparently also often a surprise to some professors.[30]

5. A more sophisticated effort to provide course and program evaluation measures has been developed at the M.I.T. Sloan School of Management, as a part of the Management of Education research project as well as for internal use in the School. These measures are based on objectives set by the faculty responsible for the courses offered; student demographics, knowledge, skills, attitudes, and expectations; and student and faculty perception of change attributable to specific courses in the academic program. The objective of further research is to develop a prototype university "management information system" to evaluate progress toward educational objectives for use by other programs and educational institutions.[31]

A somewhat similar program at the primary and secondary school level is being developed by the Center for Research and Evaluation in Applications of Technology in Education (CREATE), which operates under the auspices of the American Institutes for Research in the Behavioral Sciences, Palo Alto, California.[32] According to the director of this project, Dr. John C. Flanagan:

The development of a system of education of this type requires the formulation of detailed performance-related

---

Stanford), "Making the School Schedule by Computer: Opening New Educational Alternatives," *International Education Review,* vol. xiv, no. 2, 1968, pp. 169–181.

[30] *Time,* December 8, 1967, p. 110.

[31] This research is under the direction of Professor Arnold E. Amstutz of the Sloan School, and is now supported by grants from the Carnegie Commission on the Future of Higher Education and the Ford Foundation, covering a three-year period beginning Fall 1969.

[32] John C. Flanagan, "Functional Education for the Seventies," reprinted from the *Phi Delta Kappan,* September 1967, by the American Institutes for Research, Palo Alto, Calif. The project has partial funding and technical assistance from the Westinghouse Learning Corporation. In a subsequent paper, Flanagan called his system "Project PLAN," in "Individualizing Education," address before the American Psychological Association, San Francisco, September 1968.

educational objectives; the development of measurement and assessment devices for monitoring progress in attaining each objective; the development of guidance procedures for planning each individual's educational program in terms of detailed performance-related educational objectives; the assembly and cataloging of the modular teaching-learning units appropriate for various types of students, and the preparation of computer programs and procedures which will enable the teacher and student to use the computer effectively.[33]

A functioning model of the system was tested in 14 school districts during 1967, and it was expected that students in grades 1 through 12 would be using the new system by September 1970.

6. Computer systems for optimum allocation of university resources are being developed at Stanford, California (Berkeley), Toronto, Princeton, Michigan State, and M.I.T.[34] among others. Objectives vary, but initially they seek to optimize the use of classroom and laboratory space in scheduling students and teachers in each course, given financial resources and constraints. But analytical models might also be used for (a) strategic planning problems, assuming different parameters over time, as well as for (b) management control problems in carrying out defined objectives in shorter periods. These systems are obviously more advanced (and experimental) than the present use of computers in preparing payrolls, financial accounting and control, and student class scheduling and class rolls.

Estimates of Costs

It may be futile to discuss costs of computer-aided instruction, or costs of computer-based educational services. Most of the literature and many of the oral discussions have been concerned with *present* CAI costs (which are bound to be high in experimental programs) and with estimates of future costs per student hour under favorable

---

[33] *Ibid.*, p. 29.

[34] These are financed by grants from the Ford Foundation. The Stanford program also includes computerized information and records systems, as do many of the others. The Toronto system includes a cost simulation technique called CAMPUS (Comprehensive Analytical Method of Planning in the University Sphere).

assumptions. For example, *if* terminal costs and communication costs come down in the aggregate, and *if* large-scale applications of CAI are possible over the next 10, 15, or 20 years, *then* costs per student hour will be drastically lower than at present. More specific examples will illustrate this general point.

1. The high cost of present cathode-ray tube terminals in time-sharing computer systems is one of the reasons why Professor Donald Bitzer of the School of Education at the University of Illinois is attempting to develop the cheaper plasma-display device as a substitute terminal (mentioned earlier). He estimates that the direct *operating* costs of instruction in such a system would be about 25 cents per student hour in a system with 4,000 student terminals. But critics have called these estimates unrealistic and suggest $2.00 per student hour is more likely.[35] And these figures do not include capital costs (hardware and software) which would have to be computed for full cost per student hour over a specified period.

2. Professor Patrick Suppes of Stanford has estimated that with current technology and without involving large numbers of students, individualized work in arithmetic and in spelling could be brought to school districts at a cost of $40 to $50 per student per year (roughly 30 cents per student hour) if it were installed in reasonable numbers. On the other hand, tutorial instruction for special, remedial or vocational education, or for handicapped children, is very, very much more expensive....$3 to $4 an hour.[36]

---

[35] Wayne H. Holtzman, *Items,* p. 44. When Bitzer was questioned at the M.I.T. Colloquium Series about costs for the 25/26,000 school districts in the United States, he replied, "This will be a $50 to $100 billion a year business before we're through."

[36] Patrick Suppes, "The Computer and Excellence," *Saturday Review,* vol. L, no. 2, January 14, 1967, p. 48. Suppes used a figure of $2,000 per terminal, which he believes mass production would reduce to $1,000 per terminal, "including the cost of curriculum development and preparation." With approximately 1 million elementary school classrooms in the country, it would cost about $1 billion to install a minimum of one terminal per classroom over a ten-year period. *Ibid.,* p. 50. For alternative calculations of costs for drill-and-practice as compared with tutored systems for 100,000 students, see Clyde N. Carter and Maurice J. Walker, "Analyses," in *Costs of Installing and Operating Instructional Television and Computer-Assisted Instruction,* New York: Booz, Allen and Hamilton, 1968.

3. Even if average per student hour terminal costs were as low as $1.40 an hour, this "looms large when one realizes that a typical school system like Watertown, Massachusetts, spends only $4.00 *per year* on books for each student. The bulk of its school budget (slightly over 80 percent) goes for salaries."[37]

4. In addition to heavy initial capital costs, there will be substantial costs for the development, maintenance, and upkeep of high-quality programs (software) for CAI. "About 100 hours of author time is involved in the development of one hour of student console time for instructional applications. There doesn't seem to be any easy solution for this problem."[38] The more difficult and less-structured the subject matter, the greater these costs are likely to be. For example, a learner-controlled statistics course requires more programming effort than a structured course. To keep students interested at the college and university level, "the faculty will have to devote many hours of intensive effort creating acceptable instructional sequences; this is neither a part-time nor a trivial activity."[39]

5. If costs per student hour are to come down with widespread applications of CAI, the present lack of uniform coding standards and lack of effective language translation programs will have to be faced. One CAI expert has concluded: "Greater allocation of resources today to developing metalanguages that are completely machine-independent may be a more efficient way of spending educational development monies than to support a large number of small scale CAI projects which are not transferable to other systems."[40]

[37] Oettinger and Marks, "Educational Technology," p. 19. For further discussion of costs, see Oettinger, *Run, Computer Run,* pp. 190–200.

[38] Silberman, "Applications of Computers in Education," p. 13.

[39] Robert M. Gordon, writing in "The Forum," *Datamation,* vol. 13, no. 2, February 1967. He chided individual experiments in CAI with "neglecting the critical aspects of the systematic use of the computer outside their laboratories: the world in which each of 20,000 university students spends 15 hours per week at a 'teaching terminal' is very different from the world in which, occasionally, students make use of perhaps a dozen or fewer terminals." P. 124.

[40] Silberman, talk at American Management Association Conference, p. 13.

While actual cost estimates vary widely, the Subcommittee on Economic Progress of the Joint Economic Committee of the Congress concluded from the testimony before it, that "to receive widespread application the amortized cost of computerized instructional equipment should not exceed 25 cents per student hour in elementary schools and 50 cents per student hour for special education." In terms of initial capital costs, "somewhere between $2,000 and $4,000 per student console" (terminal) is the feasible price range "which might possibly be reached in a few years." And, "after specific curriculum objectives are established, the proper programming of such equipment would cost approximately $4,000 to provide material for one hour for an average student."[41] This was written in 1966, but at the M.I.T. Spring 1968 Colloquium Series on Education and Computers none of the speakers claimed that these objectives had been reached. As in other computer applications, the time span of achievement is always slower than the earlier predictions. But if other obstacles to widespread use of CAI can be overcome and if the present downward trend in hardware costs continues as it most certainly will, CAI will become economically feasible. However, there are many claimants on limited school budgets, and CAI is only one of them.

Some Long-Run Implications of Computer-Aided Instruction

The initial experiments and applications of CAI, as reviewed earlier, suggest the following implications on the way teaching will be done, the student's relation to the computer, and probable changes in the organization of schools and colleges.

1. Teachers will be relieved of the repetitive, structured drill-type of teaching, and possibly of grading routine papers and examinations. Presumably, when teachers are relieved of these chores, they will have more time for the creative aspects of teaching: working with individual students on difficult subject matter not programmed for

---

[41] *Report of the Subcommittee on Economic Progress,* p. 8.

CAI, discussing possible implications of points raised by students, bringing new material to the class and relating it to other areas of knowledge. CAI will probably require more imaginative teachers than before; no longer will drill work suffice to fill the class hours, particularly at the elementary and secondary school level. This may discourage some present teachers, but it may attract others because of the new possibilities.

2. In this type of CAI application, the student will have a private "tutor" in the machine and can set his own pace. At secondary and higher education levels, student interaction with the computer will be more frequent, for statistical analysis, solving problems, testing models, simulating experience, and even exploring interrelationships between areas of knowledge in an interactive sense, providing an imaginative enough program is available in the time-sharing computer.

But visionary predictions which suggest that "with this new technology we may be able to give each kid the personal services of a tutor as well informed and as responsive as Aristotle,"[42] seem a long way off. This would require voice-to-voice interaction between student and computer, with the computer "conducting a free and clever dialogue with the student," and possessing true "artificial intelligence." Anthony Oettinger, who has been concerned with artificial intelligence studies at Harvard, warns of the danger of "technical overkill." In education, he is more concerned with natural intelligence amplified by the machine rather than with the possibilities of artificial intelligence as a substitute for the classroom teacher. In his view, the blackboard is still useful.[43]

3. The possibility of teacher shortages may be relieved somewhat by CAI,[44] but a more important effect is the

[42] Patrick Suppes (Stanford) as quoted in "The Computer as Tutor," *Life*, vol. 64, no. 4, January 27, 1967. Subsequently, at the Spring 1968 M.I.T. Colloquium Series, Suppes admitted the difficulties, however, of even simpler student-computer audio communication: "This is a difficult problem. How does a computer program analyze what the student has done and then say something to help him?"

[43] Quoted in *Datamation,* vol. 13, no. 2, February 1967, p. 70.

[44] There is practically no evidence or even discussion, however, that CAI will enable teachers to handle *larger* classes, although it might seem likely.

changing of the teacher's role. In addition to having more freedom to innovate in other ways, the teacher will become part of a team of specialists, including "specialists in communications, psychology, audio-visual instruction, curriculum [design], and other subjects, working together to provide resources and instructional guides for teachers as well as students."[45]

4. There is no evidence, and there have been no predictions, that any teachers will be displaced by CAI. As poorly prepared as some teachers may be, their skills still extend beyond conducting repetitive drill-type work, which is what the computer will certainly will take over. Even the first-year college Russian Language program developed at Stanford, which purports to eliminate the need for teachers completely, would not displace any full-time teachers of Russian Language and Literature. They would be freed of beginning courses at best, with more time for advanced teaching. And it would also seem likely that beginning students may still have unstructured questions they would like to raise with a human teacher. If teachers in elementary and secondary education simply monitor the computer that now handles drill-and-practice work, and do nothing else, they will be replaced. "A happier alternative, however, is that there will be a separation of those instructional tasks most appropriate for human teachers."[46]

On the other hand, it is also probable that if CAI can handle beginning courses in mathematics, languages, and science in secondary and higher education, fewer new teachers may have to be hired, assuming the same student

---

Computer-assisted educational services, such as examination or essay grading, would also seem to help teachers to have more students.

[45] Macauley, "The Market Outlook for Instructional Technology," p. 18. For a similar view, see Norman D. Kurland, "The Impact of Technology on Education," *Educational Technology*, vol. VIII, no. 20, October 30, 1968, p. 14. Kurland believes that "the obvious increased productivity and level of professional competence of a teacher who directs a learning system and participates in the creation of effective learning materials will justify a reward more nearly commensurate with the training and ability required for the task."

[46] John I. Goodland, "The Schools vs. Education," *Saturday Review*, April 19, vol. LII, no. 16, 1969 p. 81. Dr. Goodland is dean of the Graduate School of Education at University of California, Los Angeles.

enrollments. But enrollments expand with a growing population, so that the slowness with which the new technology will spread in the next 10 to 20 years makes this a very long term possibility.

5. As in other computer applications, the student-teacher-machine interaction possibilities are exciting. It may develop that, as the student uses a CAI program in a particular field, he will have difficulties which can be met through interaction with the teacher *through* the computer, with the teacher notified of the difficulty at his own computer terminal. Professor Joseph Weizenbaum of M.I.T. has reported that "there have been many occasions when students and I worked on problems jointly while they were in Cambridge and I was at home and we were all linked through the MAC Computer" [at M.I.T.].[47]

6. There will be changes in the organization of teaching and educational institutions. The prospect of the teacher as a member of a team of educational specialists has already been mentioned in paragraph 3. School and college libraries as adjuncts of teaching (as well as research) may change with computerized information retrieval systems, but the computerized library of the future (as we shall see in the next chapter) will still be supplemented with actual books "on reserve" for courses, for student browsing, and for ready reference. The availability of national (or even international) programs and CAI systems for drill-type work and for tutorial tasks will relieve the local school or college of having to prepare these itself. For example, the programs developed at Stanford University are being used in a number of school systems; and this type of reapplication could spread. All of this assumes that eventually there will be a truly national system, with uniform programming languages, a situation which is not now the case. Regional educational utilities, similar to the time-sharing system at Dartmouth, are more likely.

7. The future role of some universities may be to innovate in developing new applications of CAI for use by

other colleges, including community colleges and junior colleges, which generally lack the staff capability to develop their own programs. Another less-likely possibility is that the so-called "learning corporations" (textbook firms allied with computer systems firms) will become the innovators, moving the major educational development functions out of the universities and into the profit-making corporate world.[48] While some educational programs have already been developed by these learning corporations, it is likely that they will also continue to work with university-based efforts.

8. More centralization of educational instruction planning and educational administration will occur in school districts with central computer systems. More or less standardized materials will be prepared for student use at classroom terminals in each school in the district, with the results being evaluated by machine and summaries of each student's progress prepared for the teacher. One prediction of this classroom of the future continues:

When it has digested the results of each class's performance, the computer composes the next lesson.... Any computer-assisted instruction worth its cost must be able to read handwriting, and interpret lengthy statements in natural language.... It will require sophisticated compilers to process and evaluate such answers, and this requirement represents the major technological obstacle standing

[48] Some of the initial bloom seems to have faded from the "learning corporation" rose, however. A survey of the experience of such firms as General Learning (GE and Time-Life), Westinghouse Learning, Raytheon Education, Xerox, CBS-Holt, and others, begins: "In virtually every case the newcomers announced their arrivals with much fanfare, high hope and brave talk. In most cases, they have subsequently encountered—or created—serious problems. So far, in fact, their results have been disappointing." Ralph Kaplan, "Learning the Hard Way: In the Knowledge Industry, Most Corporate Freshman Have Flunked," *Barron's,* vol. XLVII, November 15, 1968. Kaplan concludes, however, "it may be that these firms 'have the inside track on tomorrow's education-information markets,' " in contrast to traditional textbook companies. The survey by Arthur D. Little, Inc., discussed five "integrated systems firms" that "do not expect to have a substantial impact on the marketplace until the mid-1970's." Macauley, "The Market Outlook for Instructional Technology," p. 23. For another skeptical view about these learning corporations, see Locke and Engler, "Run, Strawman, Run," pp. 25–31. The authors, both McGraw-Hill executives, argue for the "diversity of capabilities and resources" possessed by a few of the large companies that "can produce a full array of materials and equipment, from books to computer programs to instructional equipment." P. 37.

between the experiments of today and effective computer systems for instruction in the schools of tomorrow.[49]

9. Against this trend toward centralization is the possibility that some schools may go in the direction of small, stand-alone computers rather than being a part of a massive time-sharing system. Less sophisticated hardware, software, and personnel are required; and if one computer fails, the entire system is not inoperative. On the other hand, the schools could draw programs from a central program library, developed and maintained by, say, the State Board of Education.

10. Further in the future is the educational or instructional utility system that not only provides programmed instruction through classroom or dormitory terminals in schools and colleges but also for use through terminals in the home, so that in-school as well as adult education can proceed at the individual's own pace and level of interest. By making such programs available outside of school classrooms, CAI will be more widely available and may even change the function and size of future schools. If classroom space does not need to expand to take care of all "students," teachers may function less as instructors and more as "resource" people, available for consultation by appointment with individual students as they encounter difficulties not programmed in CAI or as they yearn for interaction with a human teacher sometimes. Under such a system, teachers would need to be competent not only in the subjects covered in CAI programs but also in related and broader areas of knowledge. They would obviously be expected to help, at the student's initiative, a much larger number of students. The personal teacher-student relationship that develops in today's classrooms would give way to a more impersonal client-specialist type of relationship, perhaps not unlike that which exists between patients and doctors in a large medical clinic. This type of development, if it should occur, would obviously modify the conclusion in paragraph 4.

---

[49] James Rogers and Donald Cook, "The Computer and the School of Tomorrow," *Datamation,* vol. 12, no. 5, May 1966, pp. 41–44.

11. Centralization of CAI has dangers as well as opportunities. There is the possibility that a system based on remote information storage might make control over subject matter far easier than it is in our present society. One need only picture the use a Hitler or a Stalin could have made of a national educational information pool to understand the seriousness of this problem.... Teaching all children the same history might be all too easy and gaining control over the mind of a nation all possible unless this question is most carefully studied and intellectual freedom most jealously guarded.[50] Perhaps fortunately, the absence of federal control over education in the United States makes this less likely than in countries with highly centralized educational systems, where curriculum and standards are prescribed on a nationwide basis.

Resistances to Be Met in Introducing CAI

Some of the implications discussed earlier in this chapter suggest resistances that will have to be met as CAI is introduced beyond the present experimental level. These may be summarized briefly.

1. A national or regional CAI system will have to be acceptable to the boards and administrators of all or some of the 26,000 (or more) separate school districts in the United States. Costs of such systems must compete with the funds available (or new funds must be raised by more taxes) for new buildings, teacher's salaries, and so on. However, as suggested in the preceding section, if a school or a school district could use a smaller computer of its own, with standard programs, relatively greater progress may be made.

2. Teachers and their organizations may also resist CAI if it seems to be a threat to traditional teaching methods in which they have been trained, or if it requires considerable retraining on their part. "Teachers must be trained to use new equipment—and training takes time. Moreover, if teachers feel their prerogatives are being threatened, their

---

[50] Anthony G. Oettinger, "A Vision of Technology and Education," Harvard University Program on Technology and Society, Reprint No. 1, 1967, pp. 8–9.

resistance must be overcome."[51] Furthermore, the specialists
in the new educational technology associated with CAI are
likely to draw substantially higher salaries than teachers
are likely to get, leading to possible lack of cooperation in
the effort.[52]

3. The attempt of some learning corporations to provide a
"total educational system" is a threat to present school
systems. This is reminiscent of the talk about "total
information and control systems" in management, which
stirred management apprehensions in the mid-1960s but
has not yet been implemented. Even more serious is the
criticism that the learning corporations "have only the
vaguest notion of what an educational system is supposed
to do....There needs to be far more progress in finding out
just how children learn."[53]

4. To the extent that the CAI specialists—the systems
designers—make the same mistakes that were made in
earlier applications in management operations, there will
be the normal resistance to change by those "being
changed." This type of resistance can certainly be reduced,
as it has been in business situations, by encouraging the
participation of both teachers and school administrators in
the development of CAI applications in their own subjects
and schools. "Marathon sessions between school personnel
and systems designers provide an opportunity for each
group to confront one another, not only with their biases
but also with their particular resources for systems
design."[54] The dangers of "professionalism without
humanity" are as great here as in any other area of
computer systems application; perhaps even greater

[51] Macauley, "The Market Outlook for Instructional Technology," p. 5.
The attempt to assist teachers with specialists from outside who develop
CAI programs and curricula "is likely to meet with some resistance, simply
because it might be interpreted as incursion into what has heretofore been
strictly the educator's province—the determination of course content,
materials, and teaching methods." P. 18.

[52] Oettinger, *Run, Computer, Run,* pp. 198–199, including Table 10 on
programming salaries.

[53] Anthony Oettinger, quoted from M.I.T. Colloquium on Computers and
Education in *Technology Review,* vol. 70, no. 6, April 1968, p. 50.

[54] Silberman, talk at American Management Association Conference, p. 14.

because students as well as teachers are the ones affected by the new technology.

5. A final difficulty may be the shortage of competent systems designers and programmers for CAI. Will enough of them be available to make a real impact—with the cooperation of teachers and school administrators—in this difficult area, when there are more opportunities for immediate applications (and higher salaries) in business management, for example? There is also a lack of knowledge about how children learn, and whether any CAI can be developed which will advance the learning process significantly. Anthony Oettinger, who is quoted at the beginning of this chapter as being "depressive" about the short-run potential of CAI but more optimistic about the longer run, has put it this way: "The information available at the terminals will be prepared by people, and it is questionable whether the available people will have enough ideas and enough command of the technology to do a job good enough to interest the students."[55]

Summary

The previous discussion may be summarized with the statement that computer-aided instruction is now plagued with two major types of problems: (a) technical, including costs of hardware and software that are still too high, and (b) nontechnical problems that may prove to be even more difficult. These are elaborated in the following points:

1. Present terminal costs are too high, with the result that

A university School of Education Dean has put the same point in these words: "The demands of research and development lead the computer innovators to neglect the need for relating their work to existing practices in the mainstream of American education, particularly recent reform efforts, and to ignore the implications of their work for personnel organization and training, all potent factors in future acceptance patterns." Judson T. Shaplin, Don D. Bushnell, and Dwight W. Allen (eds.), *The Computer in American Education,* New York: John Wiley & Sons, Inc., 1967, pp. 36ff.

[55] Anthony G. Oettinger, "A Vision of Technology and Education," p. 7. He has later observed that "every attempt to introduce technological change into education has revealed how profoundly *ignorant* we still are. We know precious little about the psychology of learning, and what we know is more relevant to the laboratory than to the classroom." *Run, Computer, Run,* p. 221.

alternative hardware designs are being developed. Transmission costs also add to student hour costs. But the largest element in costs is the development of suitable programs for individualized instruction. However, all of these costs will certainly continue their downward trend over the years.

2. Computer hardware and software are not yet available for dialogue-type interaction between the student (using natural language), with the computer responding by asking questions and being helpful. Present experimental applications have been confined to the computer as a calculator, as an aid to logical thinking (through writing programs) and in routine drill-type applications, as in elementary mathematics. The computer as tutor is still limited, and the persistent shortage of good programmers acerbates the problem.

3. Present experimental applications are largely funded *outside* of school and college budgets. It is a big jump from a few studies financed by the U.S. Office of Education, or by foundations, to large-scale financing in thousands of school districts, either through their budgets or with federal support.

4. A national system is handicapped by the lack of uniform program languages and coding, by the resistance of the education establishment, and by lack of enough able, imaginative systems designers and programmers who must work with teachers and educators rather than attempt to impose systems on them.

5. Given the lack of clearly established viable CAI systems, it is probably wise to continue subsidized experimentation rather than to provide massive federal funding for any one existing system.[56]

6. It is clear from recent experience, however, that the

[56] For a supporting view, see Oettinger, *Run, Computer, Run,* p. 217: "Current attempts to integrate technology and education are dominated by faddist orthodoxy. When more and more federal money is applied to the dissemination of half-baked ideas, the return on investment is bound to be inconsequential. Rigid adherence to the dominant fad diverts both human and financial resources from both basic research and sustained development efforts necessary to evaluate and apply diverse competing ideas."

computer has the greatest immediate possibilities in the more structured subjects such as mathematics, science, engineering, and other fields in which there are structured parts (such as accounting) with some logical sequence.[57]

[57] Similar conclusions were reached by the National Council for Educational Technology in Great Britain, after reviewing the conclusions of a special Study Team that visited the United States in 1968 and prepared a report, *Computer Based Learning Systems: A Programme for Research and Development,* London, 1969. The shorter report of the National Council, headed by Professor J. Vaizey, *Computer Based Learning: A Programme for Action,* London, June 1969, recommended that the British government fund feasibility studies costing 2 million pounds over 5 years in the following fields: university mathematics, science, and medicine; learning systems in mathematics and science; training technicians in electronics; training computer specialists, student terminal development; and such special areas as application of computers to needs of less able children and to the in-service training of teachers.

2. Library Systems and Subsystems

The case for applying electronic information processing technology to the storage and retrieval of published works was first made while the computer was still little more than an experimental device. Dr. Vannevar Bush saw this need almost 25 years ago:

The difficulty seems to be, not so much that we publish unduly in view of the extent and variety of present-day interests, but rather that publication has been extended far beyond our present ability to make real use of the record. The summation of human experience is being expanded at a prodigious rate, and the means we use for threading through the consequent maze to the momentarily important item is the same as was used in the days of the square-rigged ships.[1]

Within a little more than a decade, the Ford Foundation had established a Council on Library Resources in 1956 to explore the benefits of modern technology, including the storage and retrieval of information. A study of the "library of the future" got under way in November 1961, directed by Dr. J. C. R. Licklider, who probably wrote what was the first book on the subject.[2] Subsequently, many other studies and publications, both specialized and general, have been undertaken. However, the fully computerized library system is still far in the future if, indeed, it ever can replace a library with some printed materials.

The Needs

1. The information explosion mentioned in 1945 by Dr. Bush has accelerated. Licklider has been quoted as saying that the output of readable material doubles every 10 years.[3] In the natural sciences,

where old-fashioned physics, biology, and chemistry have bred new fields like biomagnetics, macromolecular physical chemistry, and cryogenics, to name only a few, there are 35,000 separate journals published annually with over 1.5 million artlicles in them. The journals themselves are

[1] Vannevar Bush, "As We May Think," *Atlantic Monthly,* vol. 176, no. 7, July 1945, pp. 101–108.

[2] J. C. R. Licklider, *Libraries of the Future,* Cambridge, Mass.: The M.I.T. Press, 1965. The Bush quotation was cited in the Foreword to this book.

[3] *The New York Times,* January 9, 1967.

estimated to be growing in number at the rate of five to ten per cent a year; the literature in them doubling every 10–15 years.[4]

2. National as well as college and university libraries are exploding. In 1965, the Library of Congress had 40 million 3 x 5 cards in its catalog files; the New York Public Library had 2.4 million—many quite soiled and dog-eared.[5] In his paper on "A Library for 2000 A.D.," Professor John G. Kemeny of Dartmouth College said that Harvard University will have a library of more than 10 million volumes by that date, and that Dartmouth will have 2 million by then. He added, "It is clear that the cost of building, purchasing volumes, cataloging, and servicing these monstrous libraries will ruin our richest universities."[6]

3. Not only is the volume of scholarly output growing, but, as fields converge, it is often necessary for a scholar to have access to recent research in much more than his own specialized field. Furthermore, since scholarship knows no national boundaries, access to published works in other countries is essential. This will eventually require some type of worldwide information retrieval system.

Some Initial Efforts

These needs led to efforts to apply computerized information retrieval systems to library subsystems. Among the first efforts were the following:

1. About 1960, Dr. Myer M. Kessler (then at M.I.T.'s Lincoln Laboratory) began experiments with recording on computer tape certain data for each article in the *Physical*

---

[4] *The Impact of Technology on the Library Building,* a Position Paper prepared for the Educational Facilities Laboratories, New York, following a symposium of experts in June 1967. The source quoted for these data on page 4 of the pamphlet is "The Literature of Science and Technology," *Encyclopedia of Science and Technology,* Vol. 7 (1960 edition updated in 1966), New York: McGraw-Hill, 1966, p. 542.

[5] *The New York Times,* April 17, 1966. By mid-1967, the Library of Congress catalog had grown to 54 million items, indicating the rate of growth.

[6] John G. Kemeny, "A Library for 2000 A.D.," pp. 135–136 in Chap. 4 in Martin Greenberger (ed.), *Computers and the World of the Future,* Cambridge, Mass.: The M.I.T. Press, 1962.

Review for the preceding 10 years. Subsequently, he reported that some 60,000 bibliographic citations from 17 physics journals could be retrieved via teletype connected directly to the computer.[7]

2. A Medical Literature Analysis and Retrieval System (MEDLARS) has been in operation at the National Library of Medicine in Bethesda, Maryland, since January 1964. Three years later, approximately 486,000 citations from 2,400 biomedical journals were stored on magnetic tape, available for search requests from scientific investigators and members of the health professions. Some delays were reported by users.[8]

3. Computer tapes of all new English-language monographs received and cataloged by the Library of Congress have been distributed to 16 research libraries in the United States. This experimental project was begun in 1966 as Project MARC (Machine Readable Catalogue), and eventually the entire catalogue may be put on computer tapes.[9]

4. Several information retrieval systems for scientific and engineering information have been developed by firms for their own internal use. IBM's Technical Information Retrieval Center provides access to 125,000 documents, plus 10,000 annual additions, for 1700 IBM engineers and scientists. They use the system by filling out interest profiles and are then sent all articles or reports which match these stated interests. The system is able to answer inquiry searches within 48 hours.[10] North American Rockwell has developed an internal system called EDICT (Engineering Document Information Collecting Task) to

[7] The early experiments were briefly mentioned by Kessler in Kemeny discussion, *Computers and the World of the Future*, p. 169. The later report was in "Librarians Told of Computer Aids," *The New York Times*, May 31, 1967. Dr. Kessler is now Associate Director of the M.I.T. Libraries.

[8] *The New York Times*, January 8, 1967, and June 1, 1967. See also National Library of Medicine: *A Guide to Medlars Services*, Bethesda, Md.: November 1966.

[9] *The New York Times*, May 31, 1967.

[10] O. Allen Merrit and Paul J. Nelson, "The Engineer-Scientist and an Information Retrieval System," *Proceedings*, Spring Joint Computer Conference 1966, pp. 205–212.

keep its engineers up-to-date on corporate-wide design changes.[11]

Recent Efforts to Develop Computerized Libraries

With possibly one exception (Project INTREX at M.I.T.), most of the published reports of computerized library efforts indicate that these are only in the planning stage. The reality is quite different from the "vision" as projected by Professor Kemeny in the citation mentioned earlier. Among the preliminary reports are the following:

1. Project BALLOTS (Bibliographic Automation of Large Library Operation Using Time Sharing) at Stanford University has been supported by a grant from the U.S. Office of Education. This envisages a university-wide library system, which will eventually be a part of a national library communication network. A 1967 report stated that "within three to five years, some 50 terminals will be attached for remote access."[12]

2. The Yale-Harvard-Columbia medical libraries computerization project, announced early in 1965, was dropped because Harvard withdrew. Yale has continued to catalog titles, but on-line or even off-line information retrieval is still in the distant future. The data base is inititally being used for catalog card production and accession lists only.[13]

3. Beginning early in 1966, the New York Public Library was the center of a study financed by a grant from the Council on Library Resources. Among the possibilities explored was "an index stored in a computer that would flash book references on display consoles or produce them

[11] *The New York Times,* February 10, 1966.

[12] "Stanford Undertakes Big Library Project," *Datamation,* Vol. 13, no. 9, September 1967, p. 98.

[13] "Ups and Downs of Information Retrieval," *Datamation,* vol. 14, no. 1, January 1968, p. 129. Harvard's Countway Library of Medicine has continued to develop systems for its own use, as has the Harvard College Library. See Richard De Gennaro, "Automation in the Harvard College Library," Harvard Library Bulletin, vol. XIV, no. 3, July 1968, pp. 217–236. In an earlier article, De Gennaro summarized some of the major issues in library automation, "The Development and Administration of Automated Systems in Academic Libraries," *Journal of Library Automation,* vol. 1, no. 1, March 1968, pp. 75–91.

in print upon the coded request of a librarian."[14]

4. M.I.T.'s Project INTREX (Information Transfer Experiments) is, as the acronym suggests, still experimental Beginning in 1965, its announced objective was "to provide a design for evolution of a large university library into a new information transfer system that could become operational in the decade beginning in 1970."[15] The logical bases for Project INTREX were discussed fully at a 1965 Planning Conference. The "university information transfer system of the next decade" was expected to result from a confluence of "three main streams of progress":

(a) The modernization of current library procedures through the application of technical advances in data processing, textual storage and reproduction;
(b) The growth, largely under Federal sponsorship, of a national network of libraries and other information centers;
(c) The extension of the rapidly developing technology of on-line, interactive computer communities into the domains of the library and other information centers.[16]

Drawing on what is termed "the on-line intellectual community," using time-sharing computer systems based on the Project MAC experience at M.I.T., the Conference Report visualized "a time when men who work mainly with their brains and whose products are mainly of information will think and study and investigate in direct and intimate interaction with extensively programmed

[14] "Public Library Weighs Revising Outmoded Index," *The New York Times,* April 17, 1966. For a full account of this proposal, see *Library Catalogs: Their Preservation and Maintenance by Photographic and Automated Techniques,* James W. Henderson and Joseph A. Rosenthal (eds.), Cambridge, Mass.: The M.I.T. Press, 1968, Part II, Chap. B, Sec. 5, pp. 91–117.

[15] As reported in a book growing out of Planning Conference in September 1965, with participants from M.I.T. as well as other universities and institutions. See Carl F. J. Overhage and R. Joyce Harman (eds.), *INTREX: Report of a Planning Conference on Information Transfer Experiments,* Cambridge, Mass.: The M.I.T. Press, 1965, p. xv (Summary). Dr. Overhage is director of the project, which has also involved the M.I.T. Electronics Systems Laboratory under the direction of Professor J. Francis Reintjes, and the Engineering Library, the head of which is Miss Rebecca L. Taggart. Thirty-nine people are listed on the staff roster. Project INTREX is supported by grants from the Carnegie Corporation, the National Science Foundation, the Advanced Research Projects Agency of the Department of Defense, and the Council on Library Resources.

[16] Overhage and Harman (eds.), *INTREX,* p. xv.

computers and voluminous information bases." Peering
further into the future, the Report continued:

The prospect is that, when several or many people work
together within the context of an on-line, interactive,
community computer network, the superior facilities of that
network for expressing ideas, preserving facts, modeling
interaction with the same information and the same
behavior—those superior facilities will so foster the growth
and integration of knowledge that the incidence of major
achievements will be markedly increased.[17]

This type of system would be more than a computerized
library system, for it can also serve the scholar as he
prepares his research report or "manuscript." "The report
is typed just once—when the author writes the initial
draft," in the system of the future. "Because editing with
the aid of the editing program is quick and easy, and
because the current approach to computer 'understanding'
of natural language is more demanding than human
readers are for excellence of style and rigorous adherence to
stated conventions, important articles are revised and
revised." The Conference Report continues:

In the on-line community, publication is a multi-stage
process. Even while a manuscript is in preparation, it can
be as accessible to the on-line colleagues as the author
cares to make it so.
. . . .
When it is ready for more formal publication, the author
may submit his manuscript to any journal that operates
within the network.... Editors use the network in their
communications with reviewers, and that speeds up the
review process.... Publication in a good journal within the
network carries some guarantees of accessibliity.[18]

For future use of scholars, the report "is not stored all in
one place. The title, abstract, references, etc., are held in a
more readily accessible file than the body. Keyed to the
body (and to some of the figures) are sets of data. The sets
of data are stored in a data bank."[19]

[17] *Ibid.*, p. 26.

[18] *Ibid.*, pp. 36–37.

[19] *Ibid.*, p. 37. See also Appendix B, "An On-Line Information Network,"
by J. C. R. Licklider, pp. 147–155. See also Appendix G, "Data Archives
and Libraries," by Ithiel de Sola Pool, pp. 175–181. If "the storing of
basic data in retrievable and manipulable form is ... a library function,...

The publishing potential of an on-line computer system, however, was not the main thrust of subsequent work on the INTREX project, even though it was discussed at the Planning Conference in 1965. This disclaimer was specifically mentioned in the Project's March 15, 1968, Semiannual Activity Report, which reiterated what Project INTREX "really is": "It is a *program of experiments* intended to provide a foundation for the design of future information transfer systems. We visualize the library of the future as a computer-managed communications network, but we do not know today how to design such a network in all its detail."

More recent developments were reported in the September 15, 1968, Semiannual Activity Report, preceded by the director's candid comment: "As in most research undertakings, the pace has been less heroic than the vision of the planners. We had hoped to achieve the major goals of the plan by 1968, but it now seems unlikely that we shall reach that stage before 1970." One reason for the longer time required was "the decision by M.I.T. to pursue Project INTREX within the normal academic environment, rather than establish a special activity outside the regular university structure." Thus, the Electronic Systems Laboratory and the Engineering Library were the center of the experiment, which has involved faculty and students along with the research staff. Regular users of the Engineering Library are beginning to experiment with the Project facilities being developed there. At the same time, the traditional library facilities are also available, and this blend "will be characteristic of university libraries in the next decade," according to Project INTREX's director, Dr. Carl F. J. Overhage. Six months later, his Report introduction called attention to the possibility of national networks.

Information transfer networks of national scope have been increasingly under discussion, and one can see the

---

then clearly data archives also belong in the library." Pp. 180–181. Under Professor Pool's direction, a beginning in building such data archives for the social sciences, using Project MAC, is under way at M.I.T.

emergence of a pattern in which systems serving specific fields and purposes will come into existence and grow until the necessary organizational and technical steps are taken to assemble them into an integrated national network. In the meantime, the individual systems will constitute information resources of great importance to the scientific and technical community, and no research library can fully serve its users without putting these resources at their disposal.[20]

The present INTREX system is described as "an experimental pilot model machine-stored library system" and it became operational around April 1, 1969. Initially, less than 10 users had access to the interactive time-shared system under carefully controlled conditions. The main components of this pilot model are[21]

A. An augmented core-memory catalog containing key words, abstracts, bibliographical references, and other items from about 8,000 journal articles, reports, theses, and books that have been recommended by faculty members. About 9,000 items had been stored by October 1, 1969, pending reprogramming to reduce costs. Librarians and supervised student-indexers have been used.[22]

B. Information storage and retrieval programs, developed for use on the present M.I.T.-modified IBM 7094 time-sharing computer system. This will enable further experiments on storage and retrieval to be made in the context of a planned 10,000-document augmented catalog and a selected group of users. The system permits an interactive dialogue between the user and the system, narrowing down the search to documents that the user really wants or needs.[23] An "INTREX Guide" is provided

[20] Project INTREX, *Semiannual Activity Report,* March 15, 1969, p. 2.

[21] This information is based on material presented by Professor J. Francis Reintjes and his associates in the Electronic Systems Laboratory at the Industrial Liaison Symposium on "Display Technology" at M.I.T., November 14, 1968, and subsequently checked with Professor Reintjes in March and in October 1969. Fuller detail on the Electronic Systems Laboratory work for Project INTREX is found in the *Semiannual Activity Report,* September 15, 1968, Project INTREX, M.I.T., pp. 5–66, as well as in the March 15, 1959 Report.

[22] Project INTREX, *Semiannual Activity Report,* 15 September 1969, indicates the status of the program.

[23] For a sample dialogue, see Fig. B-3, September 15, 1968 Report.

for users, and there is a built-in monitoring system to observe problems users have with the system; and users can also file comments about the system.

C. A user console with a special cathode-ray-tube display. This user console had to be built in the Electronic Systems Laboratory because there were no commercially available consoles to meet the requirements of the system. Other consoles will be built subsequently, and in the meantime typewriter consoles are also used.

D. A text access program, with reproduction of photographic images of full texts either through a special microfilm printer, or a visual display on an electronic display terminal.

All of these experimental parts of the pilot model system have required considerable engineering and programming work. As one experienced librarian sympathetic to this effort and familar with it observed, "The young Turks who run the computer show have grown wiser, and the problems have proved more difficult than they anticipated."

Finally, apart from the INTREX experiment, the M.I.T. Libraries have a separate program of studies in computer-based systems. A system for the entire acquisition process was 80 percent complete late in 1969, providing status reports on acquisitions up to the cataloging step. A second system in the design stage will provide computer production of catalog cards in the M.I.T. Science Library. The third effort, computer control of the serials and journals list, is operational but a failure because the technology and the software were not ready to do the editing, alphabetizing, and merging of lists required.[24] These efforts involve what has been called the business, inventory, and housekeeping aspects of library administration. Computer applications here are likely to

[24] This information was drawn from a talk on "The Computer and the M.I.T. Libraries," by Dr. Myer M. Kessler, Associate Director of the M.I.T. Libraries, at an Industrial Liaison Symposium, "Libraries and Information Resources," at M.I.T. on March 5, 1969.

spread faster than in the information retrieval aspects characterized by Project INTREX.[25]

This section on recent developments in information retrieval concludes with the observation that progress has been slower than anticipated. However, the partially computer-based "library of the future" in large university and national libraries is probably not more than another decade away, even though books will remain in these libraries. The experience of Project INTREX has been reviewed in some detail because it suggests the direction in which these efforts are going, as well as the difficulties they face.

Some Implications of Computerized Information Retrieval Systems

Some consequences of computerized information retrieval and transfer systems have been suggested in the preceding discussion. These and other long-run implications can be summarized under the following points:

1. The library of the future "will be the central resource of an information transfer network that will extend throughout the academic community." Not only will books, periodicals, and documents in the library be retrieved by the user through the system, but he will be able to communicate with others through the network and also gain access to the university's total information resources (including data banks). "Long-distance service will connect the university's information transfer network with sources and users elsewhere."[26] This would include access not only to other libraries and to a national library (such as the Library of Congress) but also to library and information resources in other countries.

2. Before such a system is in full operation, a large

---

[25] This was the conclusion of the special conference report, *The Impact of Technology on the Library Building,* p. 10. Initial computer impacts were expected in "housekeeping chores" (order records and reports, fiscal control), to "bookkeeping operations" (buying and receiving), and finally "the computerization of the library card catalog."

[26] Overhage and Harman (eds.), *INTREX,* p. 1.

number of "expert filter" or subject-matter specialists must be attracted to assist in library-oriented activities, and thus provide the necessary intellectual input into the system.[27] Possibly full-time specialists in each field will be so attracted; but interim solutions with incentives for part-time participation may be necessary. In other words, scholars in each special field will have to be given rewards for time spent in "filtering" the voluminous specialist literature for inclusion in the system, with suggestions for cataloging, indexing, and so forth.

3. While in the long run the new system may reduce the need for *new* human librarians and library personnel such as catalogers, book selectors, and book replacers, the system will not really be *labor-displacing* in any real sense. The national shortage of trained librarians will still confront small noncomputerized libraries and compel those in the new systems to utilize those they hire more effectively. So, while this will not be their primary result, computerized libraries will also relieve library staffs of the routine and repetitive tasks of duplicating materials and preparing catalog cards for new acquisitions. It is even possible that the new computer-based system will require *new* librarians to manipulate the catalog and serve as "information brokers" or specialized aides to users.[28]

4. The main effect on library staffs, however, will be *to enlarge their responsibilities.*
Certainly, the librarian of 1975 will be less involved than now with the individual transactions between user and book.... The librarian will be of primary importance in the acquisition of new material, in cooperative cataloging, in organizing the collection, instructing users of the library, and in modifying the rules and programs to maximize the services provided to the user over the long run. The librarian will be able to operate with greater freedom by having control over advanced machinery. The librarian will be much involved with the arrangement of channels with other libraries and facilities.... It seems likely that to

[27] *Ibid.*, Appendix T, "More on the Expert Filter," by Stanley Backer, pp. 275–276.

[28] This possibility has been suggested to me by Professor J. Francis Reintjes.

be a librarian in 1975 will be very fruitful and exciting.[29]
Finally, in the vision of those at the INTREX planning
conference, "the librarian will gain immense new powers to
shape and organize the corpus of his library once the huge
burden of repetitive manual techniques has been removed."[30]

5. However, this longer-range future for library staffs will
be reached only after systems design and implementation
takes into account the sensibilities, concerns, and even fears
that present library staff people may have for the "library
of the future." In its prototype system at the Engineering
Library at M.I.T., Project INTREX has worked with the
staff of that library; and directors of the project emphasize
that great attention has to be paid to the users of the new
system, including the library staff. Indeed, one of the
objectives of the experimental computerized library is to
understand better the human reactions and interactions,
both of the users and of the librarians.

6. For the user, the computerized library of the future, as
envisioned by Project INTREX and similar systems, offers
the advantages of a man-machine interactive system. With
remote-access terminals, the scholar can query the
computer on a particular broad subfield and, by narrowing
down the topic through queries and replies, come up with
what he needs. These references can then be printed out,
either in abstract or full text form, or used in microfilm
form. The dialogue between the user and the computer is
central to this concept of on-line information retrieval and
transfer. In a fully developed system, it should also permit
cross-referencing to related fields, since knowledge is
multidimensional.

7. While "browsing" by machine seems possible under
such an interactive system (assuming that time in an on-
line system is available for this), in another sense true
browsing is not possible by machine. The scholar in
humanities or social sciences who now prowls the library
stacks looking over books catalogued in his special field

[29] *INTREX,* p. 50.
[30] *Ibid.,* p. 55.

can now open a book and sample it quickly. Will he be able to do as well in a computerized system which has, as one of its objectives, eliminating the need for enlarging book-filled libraries? Such a scholar needs time to examine carefully books or monographs; to take them to his desk or study; to look for related or conflicting theories, concepts, and facts; and to use them in his initial draft of an article or monograph of his own.[31]

Thus, there would seem to be a place for conventional libraries of some type, even in the "library of the future." Of course, certain reference works will always be available as books, and students presumably would still have access to books "on reserve" for particular courses of study. Open shelves for "browsing" by students at the college level should never be replaced by a computerized system. In short, there would seem to be a place for some part of present libraries along with the new computerized system.

8. Since many libraries will not benefit from the new systems as early as some, there is a danger in having students and other users familiar only with the new system, when they will be poorly prepared to use the "Model-T" libraries they find elsewhere. This is an additional reason why, for some period of time in the future, even a university library system may well have both the new computer-based and the traditional libraries available for different purposes by students, faculty, and other users.[32]

---

[31] See Appendix M, "How Humanists Use the Library," by John E. Burchard, in Overhage and Harman (eds.), *INTREX*, pp. 219–233. In his review of this section, Professor Reintjes disagrees. He believes that browsing is just as easy in "the machine library" as it is in the conventional one, although browsing is conducted differently in the latter.

[32] The conference held by the Educational Facilities Laboratories in July 1967 concluded that "it is unlikely that the library as a repository of books will be replaced in the near future by a computer in the basement consulted by remote consoles."

"The first phase ... will use the computer to store and retrieve highly used specialized data, probably in nonalphabetical languages, in the physical and life sciences—as is now done on a limited scale. Sometime later, perhaps within 10 years, the texts of some highly used materials selected from current science and non-science publications will be originally published in conventional print form, with a gradual increase in the production of microfilmed texts. Retrospective conversion of texts to machine readable form is not expected to any great degree for a very long

9. As noted earlier, it is important that for an extended period there be provision for user reaction to the new systems. Since the purpose of any computer-based system is to enable scholars to work more effectively, the feedback from the users will enable the system to be progressively improved. This point was extensively discussed in the Project INTREX conference. The system itself will record the experience of each user, but additional ways must be found "to keep open the informal channels of communication with the users."[33]

10. A final implication of the new information retrieval and transfer systems involves the question of reproduction of published materials. Publishers have been especially concerned about this.[34] As one publisher's representative put it at the INTREX conference, "The evolving computer technology is apt to upset the 'balance of nature' in the subtle area of the relationship between the author and his brainchild."[35] Many authors want a published end product with adequate acknowledgment and in some cases monetary remuneration. If their publications can be reproduced for users of the new system directly, there is a possibility that these users will not purchase hard copies or subscribe to journals themselves. An example of what is

---

time in the future. Therefore, the bulk of a scholar's negotiations in a library will be with books even 30 years from now." *The Impact of Technology on the Library Building,* p. 11.

[33] Appendix C, "Measuring User Needs and Preferences," by George A. Miller, in Overhage and Harman (eds.), *INTREX,* pp. 156–158.

[34] "The combination of the computer with remote copying technology will make some types of publications obsolete, such as scholarly journals, symposia, and certain kinds of reference works.... There is danger that the new technologies will have something like the same effect on books." Herbert S. Bailey, Jr., "Book Publishing and the New Techniques," *Saturday Review,* vol. XLIII, no. 24, June 11, 1966, pp. 41–43. Mr. Bailey is director of the Princeton University Press.

[35] Appendix J, "The Motivations of Authors—Intellectual Property and the Computers," by E. S. Proskauer, in Overhage and Harman (eds.), *INTREX,* pp. 199–201. For a full account of the publishers' position, and an evaluation of the problem, see *The Copyright Law as It Relates to National Information Systems and National Programs: A Study by the Ad Hoc Task Group on Legal Aspects Involved in National Information Systems,* by the Committee on Scientific and Technical Information, Federal Council on Scientific and Technical Information, Federal Council for Science and Technology, Washington, D.C., distributed by the Clearinghouse for Scientific and Technical Information, Springfield, Va., 1967.

already happening is the extensive photocopying of published and copyrighted material for individual and class use as well as for other dissemination purposes.

With reproduction facilities being an extensive part of the new system, and the further possibility that some research reports filed directly in the system may never be "published" in the traditional sense, the effect on traditional sources of scholarly publication and dissemination—to say nothing of traditional publication methods—will be substantial. It is unlikely, however, that resistances from the traditional sources can do more than to delay the eventual development of the national and international systems of scholarly information retrieval and transfer. In the meantime, there may well be extensive litigation between reproduction of copyrighted materials in computerized retrieval systems.[36]

Summary

As in the case of computer-aided instruction, there is a difference between what is possible on an experimental basis and what is likely to be the long-run vision of computerized libraries. Efforts such as Project INTREX at M.I.T. represent a possible prototype of the future, but it seems very probable that they will be more useful in the immediate future for engineering and scientific study and research rather than for the university-wide library system. When Professor Kemeny of Dartmouth College described "A Library for 2000 A.D.," in the 1962 published paper cited at the outset of this chapter, he may have been (in retrospect) overoptimistic on the time horizon.

Much more likely is the rapid spread of computer-based systems for library acquisitions, record keeping, catalog

---

[36]A book published in March 1969 by a major publisher carries the following notation: "Copyright 1969. All rights reserved.... No part of this publication may be reproduced, stored in a retrieval system, or transmitted, in any form or by any means, electronic, mechanical, photocopying, or otherwise, without the prior written permission of the publisher."

preparation, and other similar business, inventory, and housekeeping chores.[37]

The book-filled library, in the meantime, will be with us for some years to come. If computer-based information retrieval systems of the INTREX type spread, they will initially help the user of library services rather than rapidly eliminating the need for acquiring and storing published works.

[37] For a review of this experience, and a more restrained view on the spread of computerization, see Floyd E. Ellis and Carmen Ferraioli, *The Introduction of the Computer into a Library System,* unpublished Master's thesis, Sloan School of Management, Massachusetts Institute of Technology, June 1970.

3. Legal, Legislative, and Related Services

The application of computers to legal services and legislative services, to the administration of justice by courts, and to crime prevention and law enforcement is scarcely 10 years old. Most of the references to initial experiences begin around 1961 or 1962, but there is now a growing literature on computer applications and the possibilities for future applications in these related fields. The following discussion will take up each in turn.

Legal and Legislative Services[1]

The application of computers in these services has encountered some resistance for at least two reasons: (1) many law firms are small and lack the resources to utilize the new technology effectively, and (2) law by its very nature is a profession rooted in the past, and older lawyers in particular are accustomed to traditional ways of retrieving information. Furthermore, the prestige law schools have not introduced computerized information retrieval systems, although some of the less well known ones (such as Pittsburgh and Nebraska) have begun to do so. Generally, as one lawyer put it, the legal profession seems to have a "show me" attitude about computers.[2]

The Needs

Good reasons for turning to computerized legal information retrieval systems already exist, however. The low-paid "law clerk" (the recent law school graduate) is fast disappearing, with leading New York law firms now offering starting salaries of $15,000 a year, compared to $4,500 to $5,000 a decade and a half ago. The services of these new graduates in routine checking of precedents and legal references are now much more expensive than formerly. At the same time, the "information explosion" is hitting the legal profession as well as others. The flow of new court decisions, statute law, rulings by administrative agencies,

[1] This section has benefited from interviews and discussion with Robert P. Bigelow, Esq., of the law firm of Hennessey, McCluskey, Earle and Kilburn, in Boston. Mr. Bigelow is editor of the book, *Computers and the Law* (a publication of the Special Committee on Electronic Data Retrieval, American Bar Association), Chicago: Commerce Clearing House, 1966 (2nd edition, 1969). Subsequent references are to the first edition.

[2] Quoted in *The New York Times,* February 5, 1967.

and law review articles is inundating the average lawyer, law firm, or legislator. Law libraries of the Library of Congress and the universities are overwhelmed by requests for photographed copies of laws not available in the typical law firm's library.[3] Finally, law firms face the same need as business firms for reduction of office costs associated with time records, billing, accounting, and collection procedures. The computational problems in trust administration are also serious.

Early Efforts

1. One of the first publicized efforts to develop a computerized legal information system was made by Professor John F. Horty, then director of the Health Law Center at the Graduate School of Public Health, University of Pittsburgh.[4] He had started to investigate computer possibilities in 1959, and the Center got its own computer in 1962. By early 1965 he had on tape the statutes of Pennsylvania, New Jersey, and New York; and the city of Pittsburgh ordinances. The latter had been coded earlier for another computer application; incidentally, the computer analysis uncovered numerous duplications and inconsistencies. Subsequently, the appellate court and Supreme Court decisions of the Commonwealth of Pennsylvania, and all Pennsylvania statutes relating to welfare, were added. In describing his system, Horty commented: "The computer is nothing more than a meticulous, careful but not very bright law clerk. It will give you back only what you ask it for."[5]

2. The first commercial system was claimed by the Law Research Service, Inc., of New York. Started in 1964, it hoped to develop a national on-line system by 1966, but apparently this was not achieved. The system was to provide access to some 3 million case references stored in a Univac 418 system, and eventually the system was

---

[3] *The New York Times*, October 10, 1967.

[4] As reported in "Computers Do the Digging," *Business Week*, no. 1847, January 23, 1965. See also article by Horty, "The Use of the Computer in Statutory Research and the Legislative Process," in Bigelow (ed.), *Computers and the Law*, pp. 48–55.

[5] *Ibid.*, p. 50.

expected to cover all rulings in federal courts and in 15 states. Each lawyer-user had his own 10-digit code, with each inquiry costing $10 to $15, plus the cost of the Telex line and outlet rental in his office.[6] There are no published reports on the extent of use, but it is not a national system.

Recent Developments

1. After the initial efforts, the Horty program in Pittsburgh began offering lawyers an expanded inquiry service for the statute law of a number of states, plus U.S. Supreme Court decisions and some appellate court decisions. There was no charge, but users were urged to make contributions to the law school.[7] Subsequently, in 1968, Horty established a privately owned commercial service, Aspen Service Corporation. The data base available to lawyers by April 1969 included the statutes of all 50 states, the federal government, and a few federal and state court decisions. Inquiries are logged into the computer in Pittsburgh, and answers returned to the user.

2. An estate planning service designed "to bridge the information gap" between growing cases and laws and the lawyer's ability to handle them in estate planning. The system claims to do necessary calculations faster, thus providing better service to the client.[8]

3. Preparation of wills through a system developed at the University of Wisconsin in cooperation with a Madison attorney. This experimental system has a "conversational machine interviewing" program to gather data from the client in the law office. The system then manipulates the data through a will-draft algorithm to select required will

---

[6] First reported in *Business Week*, No. 1847, January 23, 1965, and subsequent notes in *Datamation*, vol. 12, no. 2, February 1966, and vol. 12, no. 5, May 1966. Another special service was to be offered by the Lawyers Center for Electronic Legal Research, which in 1967 planned to computerize Federal Tax Laws, then expand the file to include tort and contract law. The planned charge was $25 per question, using key word descriptors. *The New York Times*, February 2, 1968. Recent reports indicate this this system has not yet become commercially available as late as September 1969.

[7] *The New York Times*, July 12, 1967.

[8] This service is offered by COAP (Computer Oriented Analyses and Planning), Greenvale, Long Island, N.Y.

clauses from the library file and prints them with appropriate inserts from the interview procedure. The first test of the system showed that simple wills could be printed in about 30 seconds.[9] As in estate planning, the lawyer-client relationship is preserved, for the system is planned for use in the lawyer's office, where he can explain the results in "lay terms."

4. Trust administration—a large Boston law firm is programming a computer for this type of work, which requires complex record keeping. It is already being used for office administration, time records, billing, and so on.

5. Computers have also been used to prepare tax returns for clients and to prepare legal documents from a standardized format. They have also been helpful to some lawyers in the complex analysis of data in preparing for litigation, and this use may be expected to spread.

6. State legislative retrieval systems are being developed by several states in cooperation with computer manufacturers and some with Aspen Service Corporation.[10] Among the first states to experiment with systems for retrieving legal information for legislators were Iowa and Florida. The Iowa system claims to provide overnight delivery printouts of requested sections of Iowa laws and the state constitution, identified in the inquiry by key words and phrases. The Florida system can locate every piece of legislation filed and make available daily all actions on each bill through the previous day's session, printed out in terminals in the state capitol. The Home Rule Commission of the Massachusetts Legislature has recommended a system to provide legislators with actions on all pending laws (as in Florida), as well as codify

[9] Letter from Professor Richard W. McCoy, Director, Data Processing Center, School of Business, University of Wisconsin, September 15, 1967. Attorney William Chatterton, of Madison, worked with Professor McCoy in developing this system.

[10] States cooperating in the Aspen "experiment" will summarize research reports on about a page in a special type face, which can be read by a special optical scanning machine and stored on magnetic tape in the centralized data bank in Pittsburgh. *The New York Times,* April 7, 1968, p. 14.

existing laws.[11] This is a different system, since it will not be on-line. Other states that are reported to have computerized legal search and retrieval systems are New York, New Jersey, Pennsylvania, Ohio, Kansas, Hawaii, West Virginia, and Texas.[12]

7. Computer-aided abstracting of legal information— Project LITE (Legal Information through Electronics), U.S. Air Force. A shortage of human abstracters led to an experimental system that uses significant index words to prepare an abstract or extract of an entire body of text. The system provides an abstract that compares favorably with a human abstract, provided the author "has set form clearly and explicitly the main points" of his article.[13] The use of abstracts in this system is similar to the one developed by Professor Horty at the University of Pittsburgh.

Implications

1. Legal information retrieval systems will assist lawyers by shortening the time-consuming work in checking legal sources, if they can overcome their resistance to using machine aids. The increasingly high salaries of law school graduates may force large firms, at least, to use computer-aided legal searching systems, based on either abstracts or full texts.[14] If the system uses abstracts, young law clerks may better use their talents in preparing abstracts for the computer storage file until automatic abstracting becomes

[11] James Kelly, Chairman, Home Rule Commission, Commonwealth of Massachusetts, unpublished paper. The system is not yet operational. Indeed, Massachusetts was reported as one of the latest states to use computer systems. See *Automation in State Government, 1966-1967,* A Second Report on Status and Trends by the Council on State Governments and the Public Administration Service, Chicago, 1967. The main use reported by states is "to handle the repetitive mass of administrative transactions, tedious but inescapable, that are the chief business of modern government." P. 26.

[12] Stephen E. Furth, "Automated Retrieval of Legal Information: State of the Art," *Computers and Automation,* vol. 17, no. 12, December 1968, p. 25.

[13] Jack Sieburg in *Datamation,* vol. 12, no. 11, November 1966, p. 65.

[14] Robert P. Bigelow, Esq., has called to my attention the possibility that full text storage has the advantage over abstracts because of "its ability to retrieve by word and to retrieve actual fact situations which may be very helpful analogs to the case the lawyer has to try." (Letter, October 2, 1969.)

widespread. Some may be hired by computer utilities specializing in legal search systems, rather than by law firms as such. Probably only very large law firms would develop their own computer capabilities. According to informed people, about ten law firms had an in-house computer installed or on order by September 1969.

2. Other computer systems for estate planning, will preparation, and trust administration and real property records will free lawyers from routine and repetitive work or from tasks requiring mathematical calculations that are now performed with calculating machines much less efficient than computers. As the computer takes over these tasks, the lawyer will be freed for more constructive work on client's problems, including the personal consultation necessary to maintain the valued lawyer-client relationship. It is not clear, however, that computer systems will bring down costs sufficiently to reduce legal fees or reduce the amount of time necessary for preparing briefs or court presentations. Possibly the best that can be hoped for is that fees and legal delays will not increase as fast as they would have otherwise.[15]

3. A much more visionary view of the potential for computers on the legal profession is the following statement by a former president of the American Bar Association: "The computer will soon achieve such universal use in law research as to revolutionize the practice of law and the processes of legal systems."[16] Another lawyer in the forefront of computer applications in law has claimed that "the use of computers to retrieve legal information is the most important change in the administration of law since the advent of written law reports."[17] In another context, Merrill Flood has suggested that trial work would be speeded up because "legal information networks might.... be

[15] One computer-based service for estate administration advertises that it will justify the lawyer's charging higher fees because the client will get "better and faster service."

[16] Charles S. Ryhne, quoted in *The New York Times,* July 10, 1967.

[17] Thomas C. Plowden-Wardlaw, tax lawyer and vice president and executive director of the Lawyers Center for Electronic Legal Research, quoted in *The New York Times,* February 5, 1967.

interrogated even during trials," and consequently "the
need for complete preparation of evidence in advance
would be reduced, since the essence of every decision
process is a sequential set of steps that eventually lead to
an answer to the basic question."[18] These predictions seem
pretty far from the immediate prospects in the next decade.

4. In the near future, other impacts on the way law firms
are organized and the way in which legal counsel is sought
may be suggested. If legal information retrieval systems are
developed through computer utilities specializing in the
legal and legislative field, the law office may well be
organized differently than it is today. Smaller firms will
not need to have extensive law libraries; they can
interrogate the computerized legal centers for most
purposes and get facsimile copies of certain references after
checking the texts through visual displays as a part of the
computer system. The impact of this on law book
publishers is not difficult to foresee, although legal
problems over copyrights may well delay eventual facsimile
copies through a computer system. In any case, one speaker
at a special American Bar Association conference in 1965
made this prediction:

Eventually I foresee that we will have specialized service
bureaus located in key cities and with the law office, with
facsimile equipment, communicating into these service
bureaus or legal centers and getting results back from
them.[19]

Whether these separate centers will become part of a

[18] Report of the National Commission on Technology, Automation and
Economic Progress, Appendix Volume I, "Commercial Information
Processing Networks—Prospects and Problems in Perspective," pp. 237–
252. Professor Flood was formerly at the University of Michigan. More
recently, one writer has predicted: "In a few years, legislators, government
agencies and lawyers throughout the country are likely to accept
computerized search procedures as a standard procedure." Stephen E.
Furth, "Automated Retrieval of Legal Information: State of the Art,"
Computers and Automation, December 1968, p. 28.

[19] Raymond J. Long, "Non-Conventional Systems for the Law Office,"
Proceedings, Special American Bar Association Conference, 1965, p. 29. A
nationwide system in Belgium was in the planning stage in 1967, to service
the many one-man law offices as well as judges, "many of whom deliver
opinions without the full knowledge of legal precedents because they
cannot afford the time to look up the law in the only complete law library
in the country, in Brussells," *The New York Times,* February 28, 1967.

truly national system in the United States is less certain. Present partial systems use different descriptors (key words, phrases, and the like) to search files. Possibly a "full text" approach would permit a national system, but the question of financing the planning and implementation stages is more difficult. Given the present conservatism of the legal profession toward computer systems, a national system seems far away.

5. A final implication concerns the access to such legal information retrieval centers. Will it be confined to the legal profession only—or can others check statutes and court decsions on matters of concern to them? One example would be those concerned with public policy issues, with research on topics that impinge on the law (for example, an economist studying antitrust policies or aspects of labor law), or in fields that are closely aligned with law (for example, accountants specializing in tax matters). This is now common in law libraries and published legal services; it seems unlikely that computer utilities specializing in legal information will refuse access to laymen. But once the door is opened, the practice of law may change. Laymen may become their own "lawyers" on routine problems, despite the risks.

6. Another possibility is that centralized legal information retrieval centers, manned by a lawyer and many computer operators, may provide inexpensive legal aid services to poor people who normally cannot afford traditional legal advice in law offices. It is not difficult to conceive of such centers providing information on applicable rent laws and city ordinances, drawing up wills, processing routine legal complaints, and so forth. Centers of this type are likely to be financed by public funds in central city areas rather than by private enterprise.

7. When the implications of legislative uses of computer systems are considered, it is clear that nonlawyers among the legislators will have the same access (as they do now) to the statutes, decisions, and progress of bills through committees and on the floor as do the legislators who are members of the legal profession. These systems will

undoubtedly facilitate the work of those legislators who now have great difficulty keeping abreast of past and current legislation. Preparation of new bills will certainly be easier, especially if the computer file can be queried as to related and relevant statutes, court decisions, and other bills before the legislative body. It is difficult to see why legislators would oppose the development of such systems, but the fact that only a few states have them in operation or even the planning stage attests to the same conservatism about trying new methods which seems to characterize the legal profession. Part of this conservatism may be explained by the costliness of systems designed for a particular state.

The application of computer systems in the Executive branch of the federal government is probably further ahead than in state government administration, although state legislators have moved faster than the U.S. Congress in streamlining the legislative process with the aid of computers. In the federal government, cost-effectiveness studies in the Defense Department have drawn upon computer technology, as have other federal departments in their work, particularly in Planning-Programming-Budgeting studies. But Congress has lagged behind, even though in January 1968 the American Law Division of the Legislative Reference of the Library of Congress installed an on-line terminal system to record and store bills and resolutions introduced in the 90th Congress.[20] Other uses were visualized as an aid to Congressional deliberations, including daily printouts summarizing the previous day's congressional action, vote summaries, status of legislation pending in committees, and so on. As Congress develops these systems, and as the Executive branch develops its computer-based decision-making capability further, the question of who has access to what information will become more complex. Can the separation of powers

---

[20] John S. Saloma 3rd, "System Politics: The Presidency and Congress in the Future," *Technology Review,* vol. 71, no. 2, December 1968, pp. 23-33. This article was adapted from the author's forthcoming book, *Congress and the New Politics.* See also Robert L. Chartrand, "The Potential of Information Technology in Congressional Activity," Legislative Reference Service, Library of Congress, Washington, D.C., February 14, 1968.

concept be maintained, or will Congress "tap into Executive-based information systems.... and develop more limited information systems for its own specific requirements,"?[21]

Administration of Justice

We have noted earlier some of the resistances to computers in legal and legislative services. Similar factors account for the fairly limited application of computers in our court system. As Chief Justice G. Joseph Tauro of the Superior Court of the Commonwealth of Massachusetts has said: "We dare not proceed with undue haste even though we can't hesitate to move ahead. Law is conservative and we must anticipate opposition to realignment of court procedures and functions. So we must proceed slowly or face failures through opposition."[22] But the need for computer assistance is growing.

The Needs

Overcrowded court calendars, causing delays in scheduling which have spiraled, are compounded by present manual scheduling methods that often result in idle courtrooms and judges. Selection, time accounting, and compensation of jurors by present methods add to delays and are cumbersome. Some cases coming before courts are routine, such as parking and traffic violations. The explosion of court records has overwhelmed human clerks in many jurisdictions; present filing and indexing procedures often tie up needed court records.

For example, Judge Richard Hayden of the Los Angeles Superior Court pointed out that in 1963 civil cases totaled 800,000, yet these were inaccessible unless the court knew the case number or case title by which each was indexed.[23]

[22] Informal talk at Conference on Computers, Courts and State Government, sponsored by the Committee on Automation of the Boston Bar Association, May 17, 1968. The proceedings of this conference were published in subsequent issues of the *Boston Bar Journal.*

[23] Talk at Fall 1963 Joint Computer Conference. For a corroborating view, see Norbert A. Halloran, "Modernized Court Administration," Appendix E in *Task Force Report: The Courts,* The Task Force on Administration of Justice, The President's Commission on Law

Or, as Chief Justice Tauro put it, a better method of
retrieving data on each case is necessary for effective
judicial administration, such as referral of cases to masters,
auditors, conciliation, or assignment to specific judges. The
present method is "guesswork supported by experience"—
a manual method that often takes weeks, even months.
Finally, there is a lack of uniformity of sentencing practices
in large judicial systems, because rapid information
retrieval is lacking. When 120 judges sit in the Superior
Court of Los Angeles County, sentences for similar cases
sometimes vary, according to Judge Hayden.

First Steps

1. Initial machine applications did not involve computers.
Starting in 1964, the Los Angeles County Court system
used punched cards and an IBM electronic counting
machine to reduce its case backlog by better scheduling. It
was finally converted to a computerized system in 1968,
based on work done by the Systems Development
Corporation and the Law Research Center of the
University of California at Los Angeles. The Pittsburgh
and San Diego court systems have also used punched card
systems for scheduling trial dates in civil suits.

2. As early as 1963 Denver used computers for
preliminary scheduling of civil and criminal cases. One of
the busiest trial courts, the Supreme Court of New York
County, planned about the same time to computerize trial
scheduling. "Computer advantages over punched card
equipment for scheduling include a tighter and more
current control of information about attorney
commitments, case settlements, and courtroom
availability."[24] But they appear to be economically feasible
only in large court systems, or metropolitan areas where a
central computer can be used for other governmental
purposes.

Enforcement and the Administration of Justice, Washington, D.C., 1967.
"Court clerks sometimes view themselves more as court archivists than
court administrators, and case history sheets frequently are designed to do
little more than accommodate historical purposes." P. 164.

[24]Halloran, *ibid.,* p. 167.

Recent Developments and Plans

The available literature reviewed earlier contains more proposals for future developments than reports on existing ones. Among those possibilities, mentioned in a paper on "Court Congestion," are computerized judicial data centers, an automated civil docket, and an automated criminal docket.[25]

More specifically, the following are the areas in which computers have already speeded up court procedures or might speed them up in the future:

1. Better scheduling of court dockets, to utilize more efficiently judges and courtroom space, to prevent attorney conflicts on two or more scheduled cases, and fruitless appearances of witnesses, jurors, and others involved in scheduled cases.[26]

2. Improved preparation of court docket records, including case histories, documents, and other statistical material.

3. Rapid duplication of court forms, which are now rewritten and copied by court clerks, with possible errors as well as bottlenecks in movement of information through the judicial system.

4. Better indexing of cases, providing cross-indexing by parties' names to docket number or case number (the usual index). In 1963 it was stated that "Indexing is one of the clerical tasks that most court clerks agree ought to be mechanized. Probably from 10 to 20 courts in the country have adopted a punched card indexing system." But, a completely automated docket file would be self-indexing.... the computer printed docket would arrange case summaries in alphabetical order. Thus the two big,

[25] Halloran in Robert P. Bigelow, Editor, *Computers and the Law,* a publication of the Special Committee on Electronic Data Retrieval, American Bar Association, Chicago: Commerce Clearing House, 1966, pp. 67–72. For a similar longer discussion, see Halloran, "Modernized Court Administration," Task Force Report, Appendix E, 1968. Much of the information in this section was drawn from this report.

[26] Halloran reports that in one major city, "the trial call for one day showed 76 cases called with only 12 able to go on trial. Most of the others had attorney conflicts. Ironically, there were 14 court vacancies that day, so two courtrooms stayed empty even though thousands of aging civil cases were backed up awaiting trial." Task Force Report, p. 166.

historically separate docket records—index books and case history books—would become one. It would no longer be necessary when looking up a case to find its number first. Knowing its name would be enough.[27]

5. Better juror management, through using computerized files to select prospective jurors from a file of names; preparation of juror notices; accounting for time served; and preparation of compensation checks.

6. Assignment of counsel from a computer file of local attorneys to defend indigents or those accused in criminal cases. The Houston Legal Foundation, a legal aid organization, used a rented computer service to keep information on 3,600 practicing lawyers and programmed the machine to match an attorney's experience to the specific case.

7. Possibility of a system for assisting higher court judges in reviewing judicial appeals, based on precedents. The program would help the court search precedents.[28]

8. Possibility of a program which would (a) provide more uniformity of sentencing in a large court system, and (b) enable attorneys to "predict" the likelihood of a particular decision from a court or a judge, based on past judicial rulings there.

Some Implications

1. Computer applications in the court systems would clearly relieve clerical personnel of present routine, repetitive tasks. In fact, these would be performed more accurately, and with less delays, than at present. Case scheduling would be improved, court delays reduced, record keeping more accurate, and better access to cases provided through better indexing. An additional advantage of case scheduling by computer is that it would be *depersonalized,* not subject as humans might be, to influence in scheduling preferences or blame for errors and delays.

2. Will these computerized programs reduce the need for court clerical jobs, which are often sought because of job security or for political patronage reasons? Some may be

[27]Halloran, *ibid.,* p. 170.
[28] *The New York Times,* March 22, 1967.

displaced, although it would seem that their talents might be used to handle problems not in computer programs. Probably the number of clerical personnel hired, especially for routine jobs now handled by the computer, will be reduced. Some cost estimates of the savings from computer introductions in large urban court systems specifically mention substantial "clerical savings."[29]

3. Even if there is no actual displacement of present personnel, the fear of the new system by those accustomed to old routine ways must be considered by systems designers. As Chief Justice Tauro of the Superior Court of Massachusetts was quoted earlier as saying: "We must anticipate opposition to realignment of procedures and functions." His suggestion was that some court administrative procedures, such as civil docket entries, might first be automated, giving court personnel training in computerized procedures and involving them in the process, thus reducing their opposition.[30] This is sound advice, identical with the successful experience with computer introductions in managerial functions such as inventory control, production control, and the development of systems of management information and control.[31]

Perhaps opposition will be less from judges themselves. At least one has been quoted as saying: "We judges have no fear of automation as threatening our security of employment." Instead, he welcomed computerized trial scheduling, better preparation of court records, and a computerized index that would enable him to check precedents more quickly. If the data base is kept current,

[29] Halloran estimates that a computer center for an urban county of one million people, dedicated mainly to justice functions, would cost between $150,000 and $225,000 a year. "This would be offset by clerical savings that might very substantially reduce the cost." Task Force Report, p. 163.

[30] Talk at Boston Bar Association meeting, May 17, 1968, cited earlier in ftn. 22.

[31] "The only way to guarantee that the system will effectively serve managers as an extension of their intelligence in planning and control activities is to insist that managers influence the design. This is a very serious matter, and it cannot be left to the systems engineer without painful consequences." Zenon S. Zannetos, "New Directions for Management Information Systems," *Technology Review,* vol. 71, no. 1, October–November 1968, p. 39.

judges could also be provided with information on the status of other cases, as could attorneys interested in them. An on-line real-time system would provide this information "instantly" and could also be used for transmitting court orders, summonses, judicial notices, and other documents. It might also provide feedback to judges on what happened to guilty defendants after sentencing, subsequent paroles, and experience under parole.

4. Another implication is improved consistency of judicial decisions, to the extent that any judge could be provided with information on what other judges are currently ruling in similar cases. Prediction of judicial decisions by attorneys appearing before particular courts—now done anyway by study of such decisions and current gossip among attorneys—would be improved by better machine retrieval of the pattern of decisions in particular courts. In Superior and Supreme Courts, judicial voting patterns would be monitored, and in criminal cases, sentencing patterns. Whether or not this would improve the administration of justice, it would clearly enable attorneys to prepare their cases with better information about judicial behavior. This is a more conservative view than the following:

Computers can make calculations in a few minutes which would take a man a lifetime to complete. Thus, computers can aid lawyers and the courts obtain greater insight into the judicial process than has been possible heretofore and can aid lawyers and judges attain speedier justice for the right reasons than heretofore. Computers can help lawyers calculate the odds in their favor, and hence aid lawyers in advising clients on the best course to pursue.[32]

Crime Prevention and Law Enforcement

Police departments attempt to prevent crime, apprehend actual or potential criminals, make arrests, and handle traffic and crowds. But methods used have apparently changed relatively little in recent years, despite the use of patrol cars, radios, and central dispatch systems. In 1967,

[32] Reed C. Lawlor, "Analysis and Predictions of Judicial Decisions," in Bigelow (ed.), *Computers and the Law,* p. 60.

the members of the Task Force on Science and
Technology, appointed by the President's Commission on
Law Enforcement and the Administration of Justice, began
their study with extensive visits to police departments of
major cities, and then commented: "Our visit to the police
world was like a trip to another technological century."
Chief of Police Thomas Reddin of Los Angeles said: "We
believe we have the most up-to-date department in the
country, but our equipment has hardly changed since I
was a rookie in 1941. We are trying to fight the rise in
crime with hand-me-downs from our father's generation."[33]

The Needs

As in other knowledge-type industries, the information
explosion represented by the increase in reported crimes
and the greater volume of information on stolen property
and wanted persons (not now readily accessible in many
cases to local law enforcement officials) confronts police
departments. This has resulted in delays and even perhaps
fewer arrests and convictions. Crime prevention and arrests
appear to be a function of the rapidity with which police
patrol cars can respond to a request for help and reach the
scene of the crime. The special Task Force of the
President's Commission on Crime Prevention and
Administration of Justice found that when the response
time was 1 minute, 62 percent of the cases ended in arrest,
but when all cases with a response time under 14 minutes
were combined, only 44 percent led to arrest.

The need for a computer-aided "command and control"
system, as suggested by the Task Force, is clear. This
would reduce present delay in informing patrol cars of
reported crimes or emergencies reported to police
headquarters, aid in tracing stolen automobiles,
apprehending wanted persons, checking suspects or missing
persons, and tracing traffic and parking violators who have
ignored summonses.

---

[33] Quoted by George A. W. Boehm, "Fighting Today's Crime with
Yesterday's Technology," *Technology Review*, vol. 71, no. 2, December 1968,
p. 53. Parts of this section draw on this article.

First Steps

When Professor O. W. Wilson of the University of
California (Berkeley) was appointed Commissioner of Police
in Chicago, he reorganized the Department and began to
install a computerized command center in 1962.
Subsequently, the system has been developed with third-
generation computers to permit operators at computer
consoles to maintain instant communication with the
patrol cars in particular areas. Policemen can get a 10-
second reply on suspected stolen automobiles or on wanted
or missing persons, from information stored in the
computer's random access files. The system also provides
daily reports to each of 21 field commanders on crimes by
type and location in the city. Each field commander can
then evaluate his situation relative to all others, and field
administrative decisions can be made better.[34]

Another relatively early development was in the New
York State Police system. A computer file for storing
registration numbers of stolen cars and stolen license plates
was developed and tied in with consoles in municipal
police departments and county sheriff's offices. Answers
were provided in 60 seconds.[35]

Later Developments

In addition to the further refinement and expansion of the
Chicago system, the following have been reported more
recently:

1. A New York City system which reduces the delay in
relaying emergency calls from headquarters to patrol cars
from 90 seconds to 20 seconds. Police Commissioner
Howard R. Leary stated: "Our aim is centralization. More
and more emphasis is put on instant communications for
tactical purposes."[36] The city has also contracted with a

---

[34] Based on reports in *Business Week,* no. 1898, January 15, 1966;
Datamation, vol. 13, no. 7, July 1967, p. 52; and Boehm, "Fighting Today's
Crime" (photographs).

[35] *Datamation,* vol. 11, no. 12, December 1965. For a graphic illustration
of the case of a Maryland State Policeman's apprehension of wanted
criminals through a suspicious out-of-state parked car, determined to be
stolen through a 60-second inquiry of a computer file, see Boehm,
"Fighting Today's Crime," p. 59.

[36] *The New York Times,* August 30, 1966.

private bank to receive parking fines, and for the use of computerized system that checks the bank's record of fine payments with an outstanding list of summonses and then issues new ones.[37]

2. Alameda County, California, has a Police Information Network (PIN) in an on-line real-time system covering 4 million people (including the city of Oakland). This is also tied in with the Statewide Theft Inquiry System in Sacramento.[38]

3. A Pattern Recognition and Information Correlation System (PATRIC) has been developed by the Systems Development Corporation for the Los Angeles Police Department, to assist in crime detection. While the department is apparently organized in decentralized field commands, crime data can be processed on a city-wide basis and there is a real-time inquiry system for wanted individuals.

4. The F.B.I. has developed a National Crime Information Center that maintains a computerized file of stolen cars and wanted criminals nationally. State and local systems can tie into it.[39]

5. Philadelphia has recently established a police computer unit and is planning to schedule patrol car assignments on the basis of a detailed crime forecast covering each part of the city for each hour. With the help of the Franklin Institute, a computer program is being developed to make such predictions automatically.[40]

6. Finally, one major proposal of the Task Force of the President's Commission is still to be implemented in any city. This is "a completely automatic computer-controlled system" for dispatching patrol cars. After a clerk informed the computer of the nature and location of reported trouble, the program would automatically radio commands to the nearest car or cars, cutting response time to a minimum.[41]

[37] *Business Week,* no. 1972, June 17, 1967.

[38] *Datamation,* vol. 13, no. 3, March 1967.

[39] *The New York Times,* January 28, 1967.

[40] Boehm, "Fighting Today's Crime," p. 58.

[41] *Ibid.,* p. 57.

Implications

1. If most police work is characterized by methods that have changed very little over a generation, then computers will drastically alter it. But it is a reasonable prediction that some police will be relieved of clerical work and freed for the work for which they are presumably trained: preventing crime and other law violations, and apprehending actual or potential law violators and criminals. Others will be freed for traffic control duty.

2. There will be more centralization of "command and control," but if better and more rapid information is provided to field commanders (as in the Chicago system) and to the patrolmen in cars or on the beat, then they too have their jobs made *more* effective, not less effective. No computer will apprehend a criminal or prevent a crime; but it may help the man do this in a true man-machine relationship that is likely to be superior to any previous system.[42]

3. Computerized systems will also result in a better deployment of a costly resource—policemen, who represent as much as 85 percent of some police budgets. But if more "money" is spent for computer hardware, software, and human programmers, the budget proportions may shift, as in Chicago, to 30 percent for equipment and 70 percent for personnel. Old-line policemen will have to get used to a new breed: systems designers and programmers who will become more important in the future. As one speaker at the Fall Joint Computer Conference in 1966 put it, [the problem] of implementing an effective systems analysis into the urban management context will be two-fold: (1) to obtain cooperation for a full, rather than a piecemeal, systems effort; and (2) to devise a communication and control system that adequately reflects organizational objectives.

But there is likely to be resistance by the public manager, including some police commissioners, "whose natural

---

[42] An IBM advertisement puts it this way: "Computers don't make arrests. But in a split second, they can give the policeman his most effective weapon against crime—information."

aversion to change is reinforced by statute, code, administrative, and civil service regulations."[43]

4. A further source of resistance may be the fear that greater centralization of files will present a security problem. According to *Business Week*, "The FBI is appalled by the prospect that organized crime might sabotage a national computer, or dig information out of it for blackmail."[44] While this may seem farfetched, the fact is that computer systems with codes for limited access have been entered by unauthorized but skillful personnel. This question of "privacy" will be discussed in more detail in Chapter 5, dealing with national and centralized local banks.

Summary

The common threads in the four areas reviewed in this chapter may be summarized as follows:

1. Computers have already assisted information retrieval and reproduction in legal and legislative services, administration of justice, and crime prevention and law enforcement. Despite the conservatism of many practitioners in these fields, the information explosion will force them to turn more and more to electronic data processing in order to cope with their problems.

2. Information technology specialists will reduce opposition to new introductions to the extent that they involve the people affected in the preliminary discussions leading to the design of new systems, and thus help to allay their fears of new ways of doing traditional tasks.

3. It is unlikely that professionals will be displaced by computers; instead their skills and talents will be better utilized as they are relieved of routine tasks. The possible exception is court clerical staffs, whose hand preparation of cases, indexes, schedules, and the like, may well be replaced

[43] Richard B. Hoffman, *Proceedings* of Fall Joint Computer Conference, 1966, p. 524.

[44] "Computers Play Cops and Robbers," *Business Week*, no. 1898, January 15, 1966, p. 138.

by computers. While it is unlikely that present personnel will actually be displaced, new hiring will certainly be reduced.

4. The speed of the computer will provide rapid access to cases by lawyers and judges, to laws and legislation in process by legislators, to offenders and wanted persons by crime prevention and law enforcement officials.

5. All of these developments are likely to change the organization structure of law offices, legislative services, juducial systems, and police departments. Information and access to information will be more centralized, but professional people with better information may be able to act more effectively in pursuit of their objectives than they were in the precomputer age.

4. Medical and Hospital Services

As in other areas examined in the preceding chapters, the actual and experimental application of computers to medical and hospital services is moving rapidly. Keeping up-to-date on developments in this field is often as difficult as it is in the other knowledge-based fields. An editorial in the special 1966 issue of the *Journal of the American Medical Association* on computer applications posed the question: What is the present status of the computer in medicine? The honest answer to that question is, of course, that we do not know. In common with publications in all fields of human knowledge, medical literature is old the day it appears in print.[1]

In attempting to assess what has happened, it is important to remember the *caveat* suggested by Dr. G. Octo Barnett, Director of the Laboratory of Computer Science at the Massachusetts General Hospital in Boston:

I am concerned with the scientific integrity of the approach that allows a broad statement that the computer can do tasks X, Y, and Z when even a superficial investigation would reveal that X can be done only on a limited demonstration basis in an artificial environment, Y is being seriously considered as an area to be programmed three years hence when system "...." is fully functioning, and task Z looks like a challenging problem in information processing and wouldn't it be nice if we could get a National Institute of Health grant to carry out a research project. *The failure to discriminate between present reality and future speculations has been one of the major causes of frustration and misunderstanding in the medical applications of computer science.*[2]

The Needs

A review of the literature on computer applications in medical and hospital services indicates the following needs that have called forth these efforts:

[1] *Journal of the American Medical Association,* vol. 196, no. 11, June 13, 1966, p. 1014.

[2] In *Report to the Computer Research Study Section,* Research Grants Review Branch, Division of Research Grants, National Institutes of Health, on Computer Applications in Medical Communication and Information Retrieval Systems as Related to the Improvement of Patient Care and the Medical Record, September 1966. (Also contains an annotated bibliography.) (Italics added above.)

1. The information explosion resulting from increased records for present and past patients means that professional hospital personnel may spend a third (or more) of their time on information processing. Much of this is routine clerical work with manual methods which have been used for many years.[3] The consequences of the record-keeping explosion are dramatically shown in the experience of the Massachusetts General Hospital:

The Medical Records Department now stores 1,350,000 records dating from 1937. During an average day, 150 new patient records are issued and over 4,000 demands for existing records are made.... The various laboratories perform 1,000,000 procedures per year.... Each time a patient is admitted, pertinent information is sent to some 30 different areas. It is estimated that on an average day, some 5,000 doctor's orders are written and the nursing service administers over 30,000 drugs and treatments. It is probable that at least 50,000 separate items of information are entered into patient records each day, or almost 20,000,000 separate items each year. The problems created by the large bulk of information processing are greatly magnified by the complexity of the data flow. For example, there are 24 different laboratories in the MGH which perform over 300 different laboratory tests involved in routine patient care.... The manual transformation from the patient domain (the doctor's order book) to the time domain requires many hours of clerical work on the part of the nursing staff. For example, a nurse in each care unit may spend 4 hours each day on bookkeeping activities concerned with the ordering, administering and recording of medications."[4]

2. There is a chronic shortage of all kinds of medical and hospital personnel, and this has recently been accentuated with the advent of Medicare. One expert in medical economics has estimated that the number of physicians will increase to 362,000 by 1975, a 19 percent growth over 1965.

---

[3]"It is probably true that many of the record keeping methods we use (in hospitals) are somewhat archaic and represent the carry-over of practices developed 30 to 50 years ago." Jordan Baruch and G. Octo Barnett, quoted in *Datamation,* vol. 11, no. 12, December 1965, p. 30.
[4]G. Octo Barnett, The MGH Report, Hospital Computer Project, February 1966, pp. 14–17.

Assuming no increase in physician productivity, but with a continuation of the annual addition of 1,600 foreign-trained new licentiates, there could be an increase in the number of physicians' services per person. This increase, however, would not be sufficient to meet the expansion of demand resulting from higher incomes.[5]

Perhaps even more serious is the shortage of nurses, medical technologists, and other types of paramedical personnel.[6] To some extent the lower salaries, long hours, night shifts, and other conditions of employment which are less favorable than those available in other skilled occupations may account for the "shortages." Whatever the reasons, the existence of unfilled manpower vacancies in hospitals and medical centers continues. Research studies of the health manpower field are proceeding in a number of places, and "action programs" are proposed at federal and state levels. New medical schools are being established. But present shortages are not likely to be alleviated within the foreseeable future.

3. While the practice of medicine has required more sophisticated information in greater quantities, professional medical personnel have less time to process it because of the shortages already mentioned. Thus, the possibility of human error is probably increased. One hospital reported that there were 5 percent errors in all of the manual processing of the administration of medication through the hospital pharmacy. It has been claimed that even the doctor's memory needs an "electronic crutch" through computerized medical information retrieval or through computer-aided diagnosis, discussed later. The information explosion has swamped the medical profession, sometimes

[5] Rashi Fein, *The Doctor Shortage: An Economic Analysis,* Washington: The Brookings Institution, 1967, p. 139. Fein points out that in the past "productivity changes were necessary to keep up with the growth in demand," including the use of antibiotic drugs, use of auxiliary personnel, shift to office visits, and changes in the organization of the physician's office. In the future, more group practice may also be helpful. Fein does not discuss the possible increase in productivity through the use of computer technology.

[6] *Technology and Manpower in the Health Service Industry, 1965–75,* Manpower Research Bulletin No. 14, U.S. Department of Labor, May 1967, especially pp. 18–24.

with serious consequences.[7] The workload of lab
technicians in hospitals is increasing each year, but they
must spend as much as 2 hours daily on clerical work,
with possible errors in transcription. Thus, the opportunity
for computer-based information processing is present,
although the task of developing a computerized system is
never easy.[8] Also, with the present more-powerful drugs,
mistakes can be more costly. Using the wrong drug or the
wrong amount is more likely to be fatal than formerly.

4. Finally, the process of diagnosis itself is time-
consuming. Patients may not immediately be referred to
the right specialist, with consequent loss of time to doctor
and patient. Then the actual diagnosis may take much
longer if tests are spaced out and if a number of specialists
have to be consulted. The adminstrator of the Bellevue
Hospital in New York City is quoted as saying: "If you're
acutely ill, we can handle you. But if you've got diagnostic
problems, it can take six weeks to get a diagnosis."[9]

Initial Efforts

The first computer-applications reported in the literature
cover medical records, hospital administration,
electrocardiogram analysis, and medical research. All of
these are continuing, so that distinctions between first steps
and recent applications are somewhat hazy.

---

[7] According to a *New York Times* editorial,"Many people die needlessly of
Hodgkin's Disease, a cancer of the lymphatic system, because their doctors
are ignorant of the major advances in treatment made during recent
years. . . . Presumably there are many other diseases in which the gap
between the most effective treatment known and that actually received by
many patients is very wide indeed. One reason is that even physicians who
seek to keep up with advances in medicine are swamped by conflicting
demands of an overly busy practice and the information explosion in their
field." *The New York Times,* February 19, 1969.

[8] Two doctors reported in 1965 that one such computerized system was
discontinued because of errors in input, excessive time requirements on the
medical residency staff, unacceptable time lags, and, above all, a cost
much greater than originally estimated. H. W. Baird and J. M. Garfinkel,
"Electronic Data Processing of Medical Records," *New England Journal of
Medicine,* vol. 272, 1965, pp. 1211–1215.

[9] Dr. R. A. Wyman, quoted by Dr. John F. Davis, "Computers and
Medicine," *International Science and Technology,* no. 60, December 1966, p. 46.

Medical Records

By 1965 about 200 large hospitals either had installed computer systems or had computers on order for storing some medical records and for other administrative purposes.[10] Some of these were probably "experimental" and research-oriented, as was one of the most publicized: the Massachusetts General Hospital project under the direction of Dr. G. Octo Barnett. It began in 1962 with the assistance of Bolt Beranek & Newman Inc., a Cambridge consulting firm. The purposes of this project initially were to (1) "increase the rapidity and accuracy of collecting, recording, transmitting, retrieving and summarizing patient care information," (2) "decrease the amount of routine paper work required of the nursing staff," (3) "arrange and consolidate information for more effective and efficient utilization by the medical staff," and (4) "store large amounts of complex medical information and contribute to clinical research by facilitating rapid and easy retrieval and analysis of stored information."[11]The first MGH "developmental-experimental" project was the use of a small time-shared computer to process drug orders in the hospital's pharmacy. The computer program included correct formulas, dosages, and other directions, so that orders transmitted by doctors or nurses were checked for accuracy before being filled. Doctors or nurses could override the dosage limits, but only on notification by their names. However, the former noncomputerized system continued in parallel with the new system, with the result that the staff withheld "full support and utilization of the experimental system in favor of the old-fashioned, time-tested one."[12]

---

[10] *Technology and Manpower in the Health Service Industry, 1965–75,* p. 46. For an account of conversational computer interviewing of medical patients to obtain medical histories, see Werner V. Slack, G. P. Hicks, C. E. Reed, and L. J. Van Cura, "A Computer-Based Medical History System," *New England Journal of Medicine,* vol. 274, January 27, 1966. Dr. Slack is Professor of Computer Science and Medicine at the University of Wisconsin. The system is now reported to be in operation, using a cathode-ray tube for showing questions to the patient, who responds by pressing certain buttons.

[11] MGH Project Status Report, February 1, 1966, p. 1.

[12] *Ibid.,* pp. 24–25. The total staff of the original project numbered 71,

The computer project at the Tulane University School of Medicine, directed by Dr. James W. Sweeney, began pilot studies in 1961 looking toward electronic storage and retrieval of patient's medical records. These included records for patients in cardiac surgery, cancer detection, obstetrics, gynecology, orthopedics, pediatric cardiology, and psychiatry. By 1966 there were more than 40,000 individual case histories in Tulane's computer data bank. Information was submitted by physicians on self-encoding worksheets for each patient. To make subsequent information retrieval for the physician easier, a natural language (Meditran) was developed to permit the physician to use words to specify what information he wanted.[13]

Hospital Administration

Accounting, payrolls, and dietary administration have been natural computer applications in hospitals and medical centers. The Minnesota Hospital Service Association provides a computerized service to 180 hospitals for all of these purposes, and eventually for medical records.[14] Other groups of hospitals in New Jersey, and in Peoria, Illinois, Falls Church, Virginia, and Wilmington, Delaware, among others, are sharing computers for accounting purposes. Patient billing has also been speeded up by computerized systems. The Abbott Hospital in Minneapolis, for example, draws on the central file just mentioned for patient's records, and gives the patient his bill "in a matter of seconds, whereas formerly it took considerable time for the office staff to look up all the individual charges."[15]

---

34 of whom were from the hospital and 37 from the consulting firm. It was financed by grants from the National Institutes of Health, the American Hospital Association, and the American Heart Association.

[13] "Packaging Patient Information," *Hospital Physician,* vol. 2, no. 9, September 1966, pp. 45–46.

[14] "Hospitals Share Computer Through Communications," *Systems,* vol. 8, no. 2, February 1967, pp. 12–14. Hospital administration is apparently still the major application of computers, despite the interest in more recent experimental applications. See J. Peter Singer, "Computer-Based Hospital Information Systems," *Datamation,* vol. 15, no. 5, May 1969, pp. 38–45. This is an up-to-date survey of recent developments.

[15] "Hospitals Share Computer Through Communications," p. 14.

Electrocardiogram Analysis
George Washington University Hospital in Washington, D.C., began in 1963 to develop a computer program for analyzing abnormalities and deviant patterns in electrocardiograms. The Veteran's Administration began a similar effort before 1965. The Mt. Sinai Hospital in New York programmed a computer before 1966 to recognize and interpret rhythm changes in the heart's beat.[16]

Research
As in other types of scientific research, the computer's facility for rapid data processing has relieved medical research workers of much of the drudgery in their work and has speeded "critically important experiments."[17] As noted earlier, a number of the early computer applications in medical and hospital services could also be termed "research."

Recent Applications

Some of the initial projects have continued; these and additional computer applications will be summarized under the following headings: diagnosis and treatment, information retrieval systems, planning and managing complex medical and surgical procedures, hospital administration, and medical education.

Diagnosis and Treatment
In an early summary of computer-aided medical diagnosis, four general areas were listed as relevant: (a) "the communication of information about the patient to the physician, (b) comparison of patient information with available medical information, (c) diagnostic decision making, and (d) treatment of the patient."[18] A more

[16] As reported variously in *Datamation,* vol. 11, no. 12, December 1965, *Technology and Manpower in the Health Service Industry, 1965–75,* p. 40; and *The New York Times,* March 3, 1966. The pioneering George Washington University program was developed by Dr. Cesar A. Caceres and two colleagues. Dr. Caceres subsequently became Director of the U.S. Public Health Service Medical Systems Development Laboratory in Washington. *The New York Times,* December 7, 1967, p. 42.

[17] *Business Week,* no. 1923, July 9, 1966, p. 142. This article has a summary of early uses on computers in medical research laboratories.

[18] Lee B. Lusted, "Computer Techniques in Medical Diagnosis," Chapter

visionary and optimistic view of the future was outlined by another writer in 1965:

Diagnostic assistance by computers is an attractive potential application.... In a typical exchange with the computer, a physician might type in a few symptoms, and the computer would respond by printing out a list of possible diseases. The physician might then ask why a particular disease appears on the list, and the computer would supply a number of possible cause-and-effect relationships. The physician could then ask for more information about a particular causal path, examine the logic, and agree or disagree with the computer's response. Searching in this way, the doctor could make a logical examination of all the reference possibilities stored in the machine....[19]

Despite this optimistic view, a 1966 report concluded that "there has been little operational success in the area and most of the work has been either theoretical, developmental or sharply limited."[20]

Among the more recent *experimental* attempts to develop computerized systems to assist doctors in medical diagnosis are the following:

• A sequential approach to computer-aided diagnosis is being developed at the Massachusetts General Hospital by Professor G. Anthony Gorry of the Sloan School of Management in collaboration with Dr. G. Octo Barnett, Director of the Laboratory of Computer Science at the hospital.[21] Their experimental "sequential diagnosis" is designed to correspond to the sequence of steps a doctor

---

12 in Ralph W. Stacy and Bruce D. Waxman, *Computers in Biomedical Research,* vol. I, New York: Academic Press, 1965, p. 321.

[19] Evion C. Greanias, "The Computer in Medicine," *Datamation,* vol. 11, no. 12, December 1965, p. 27.

[20] Dr. G. Octo Barnett in his MGH Project Report, September 1966, Appendix, p. 25. The one exception to this generalization was, he noted, "the automatic classification of electrocardiographic abnormalities" by computers.

[21] G. Anthony Gorry and G. Octo Barnett, "Sequential Diagnosis by Computer," *Journal of the American Medical Association,* vol. 205, no. 12, September 16, 1968, pp. 849–854; and G. Anthony Gorry, "Modelling the Diagnostic Process," M.I.T. Sloan School of Management, Working Paper 370-69, February 1969. A brief account of this approach was also reported in *The Technology Review,* vol. 70, no. 6, April 1968, p. 51.

uses in diagnosis, as opposed to present computer diagnostic systems which start out with all the relevant data, including tests which may be unnecessary and costly. The new system involves three parts: (1) the information structure constituting the medical experience available to the program, including probabilities of certain diseases occurring with certain symptoms, and costs of various tests and misdiagnoses; (2) the inference function, which uses Bayes rules to update a probability distribution for the disease in question, as the sequential interaction of the doctor with the computer in English conversation proceeds in real time; and (3) the test selection function, which selects one of several decision alternatives corresponding to each potentially useful test and one corresponding to the cessation of testing. This step takes into account the current view of the problem (as seen from the inference function), the cost of the test, and possible test results. The test selection function determines the best test to perform at a particular stage in the diagnosis, as contrasted with other computer-aided diagnostic programs that *begin* with a number of possibly helpful and often costly tests.

This sequential diagnostic program has been tested in the diagnosis of bone tumors, congenital heart disease (35 different types), and recently, acute renal failure. These programs have been developed on M.I.T.'s pioneer time-sharing computer, Project MAC. Preliminary experience supports the superior value of sequential-decision making in computer-aided diagnosis, although the researchers state that more extensive evaluation will be necessary.[22] One additional value of the system may be that paramedical personnel such as nurses could query the program and know when a patient should be referred to a specialist on the disease.

Professor Gorry is also working with the New England Medical Center of Tufts University in developing similar computer-aided sequential diagnostic programs in

[22] Gorry and Barnett, "Sequential Diagnosis by Computer," p. 854. Professor Gorry is extending the renal failure study to deal with the assessment of therapeutic strategies when significant risk is involved.

collaboration with doctors who help revise and test the programs. These may later be available to doctors throughout the region to assist diagnosis of certain diseases.
• Computer-aided electrocardiographic analysis of heart patients is being extended over wider geographic areas. Early in 1969, a computer at Mt. Sinai Medical Center in New York City was available to doctors in West Virginia through a project carried out jointly by Mt. Sinai, the West Virginia State Health Department, and the Cro-Med Bionics Corporation. The program is still experimental, since the EKG readings transmitted to the New York computer by special modulated signals over the telephone are being checked by mailed magnetic tapes and by independent EKG analysis. In the past, West Virginia hospitals have waited two weeks for an analysis by distant cardiologists, and the computer-aided system promises two-minute results by telephone to the waiting doctors.[23]
• A computer has been teamed with a device called a scintiscanner by doctors at Long Island Jewish Hospital to find thyroid and brain tumors directly in patients, and to pinpoint the location and size of the growth. The computer analyzes the x rays, by a technique derived from military uses to examine aerial photographs for enemy troop concentrations. The computer can detect shades of gray in the x ray, indicating tumors that visual examinations may miss.[24]
• On-line computer monitoring of heart and lung conditions of patients in intensive care units has been developed at the Pacific Medical Center in San Francisco, as a joint project with IBM. It is claimed to be more than automated record keeping, because it "is aimed at spotting potentially dangerous conditions early enough in their development cycle to correct them easily and minimize their medical effect on the patient."[25] The system, which

[23] "Computer to Aid Heart Diagnosis," *The New York Times,* December 8, 1968, p. 59.

[24] "Computer Helps to Detect Tumors," *Boston Sunday Herald-Traveler,* March 2, 1969, Section 4, p. 3.

[25] James O. Beaumont, "On-Line Patient Monitoring System," *Datamation,* Vol. 15, no. 5, May 1969, pp. 50–55.

first went into operation several years ago, also provides for the rapid access to data needed by medical personnel to take the corrective action. Skin temperatures and blood pressure are also monitored by the system.

• A Computer-Aided Diagnosis System (CADS) has been developed at the University of Missouri Medical Center. It uses Bayesian methods to calculate the probability of certain diseases, given particular symptom levels. Early in 1969, the system provided for the simultaneous use of up to eight CRT terminals.[26]

• A matrix-type diagnostic computer has recently been patented in the United States by the Nippon Electric Company, Ltd., of Tokyo. According to a published account, a similar computer has been used for some time in the Tokyo University Hospital and 50 other Japanese hospitals. Symptoms are linked with diseases in the computer's memory, and weight is given to the degree of certainty associated with symptoms for a particular disease. When buttons are pressed on the matrix, "an ammeter indicates the most likely disease." There is some doubt, however, whether this will really aid doctors in diagnosis.[27]

Information Gathering and Retrieval Systems

Computer-aided diagnostic systems do involve information gathering and retrieval, but more common uses of computers simply provide the doctor with access to computer-based information. Some of these involve collection of medical histories, laboratory tests, and other related information. Others draw on information in medical libraries, or attempt to develop national systems for specialized medical or technical data retrieval. Among the recent developments in these types of applications are the following:

• Patients are given self-administered questionnaires by

[26] Mimeographed paper from the Center, March 1969.

[27] "Japanese Company Promotes Diagnosis by Computer," *The New York Times,* August 31, 1968, p. 42. The computer has circuits for 40 diseases and 40 symptoms. It is obviously quite different from the "sequential diagnosis" developed by Gorry and Barnett, especially since *The New York Times* further states: "The company says its operation does not require professional knowledge of medicine or electricity; the patient himself could push the buttons."

the Kaiser Foundation Health Plan in the San Francisco area, with the answers, along with routine test results, fed into the computer. This information can then be used by the physician in his subsequent examination of the patient.[28] This experience seems to be the prototype of the concept of "automated multi-phasic health screening (AHMS)" which is claimed to streamline the "time-consuming, office bound physical examination" by reading, processing, and interpreting past medical records, analyzing other tests, and producing a printed report for the company or family doctor.[29]

• The Mayo Clinic has used a computer analysis of the results of the Minnesota Multiphasic Personality Inventory, to provide the doctor who is not a trained psychiatrist or clinical psychologist with a clinical evaluation of the test results on a particular patient.[30] The computer center at the Rockland State Mental Hospital in New York "enables psychiatrists to maintain accurate, standardized medical histories; someday they may also help the diagnosis." The system includes pencil notations on forms that describe a patient's behavior, and the computer then stores this information to provide the psychiatrist later on call with a full patient history in straight sentences.[31] The Lahey Clinic in Boston is also using this system.

• A "symptom questionnaire" sent to patients prior to their visit, has been developed at the Lahey Clinic in Boston by Professor John F. Rockart of the Sloan School of

[28] As reported by Paul Armer in Appendix Vol. 1, p. 225, of *Technology and the American Economy: Report of the National Commission on Technology, Automation, and Economic Growth,* Washington, D.C., 1966. For another report, see M. F. Collen, "Periodic Health Examinations Using an Automated Multitest Laboratory," *Journal of the American Medical Association,* vol. 195, no. 10, March 7, 1966, pp. 142–145.

[29] "Electronic First-Aid for the Busy Doctor," *Business Week,* no. 2040, October 5, 1968, pp. 156–158.

[30] Lusted, "Computer Techniques in Medical Diagnosis," p. 322. Also see, Howard P. Rome, M.D., William C. Menninger Memorial Lecture, "Psychiatry: Circa 1919–1969–2019," American College of Physicians, Spring Meeting, Chicago, April 25, 1969.

[31] Thomas Fleming, "The Computer and the Psychiatrist," *The New York Times Magazine,* Sunday, April 6, 1969, p. 47.

Management at M.I.T., working with Clinic staff.[32] It is useful in determining which specialists a patient should see first, and in providing the specialists with a partial "work up" of the patient's medical history. The system is still being developed, as attitudinal studies are being made of the experimental program. Those doctors who have been most involved in the development of the system are most likely to use it and feel that it has been helpful to them.[33]

• The Massachusetts General Hospital in Boston is also working on an automated collection of medical histories of patients in the ambulatory clinic, using time-sharing terminals.[34] This approach requires that the patient be at the hospital, and it is more costly than the patient questionnaire used at Lahey Clinic. While it provides the physician with an on-line medical history, it does not permit advance scheduling of patients to specialist physicians. The system does include automatic ordering of particular laboratory tests and minimal automatic differential diagnosis of those medical histories specifically oriented toward a complaint, such as a chest pain, a headache, and so on.

• A laboratory test reporting system is the largest ongoing research project of the Laboratory of Computer Science at Massachusetts General Hospital, and is claimed to be the largest of its kind in any hospital in this country.[35] The project began with the Chemistry

[32] John F. Rockart, Philip I. Hershberg, Jerome Grossman, and Richard Harrison, "A Symptom-Scoring Technique for Scheduling Patients in a Group Practice," *Proceedings of the Institute of Electrical and Electronic Engineers* (special issue on Automated Health Care), vol. 57, no. 11, November 1969.

[33] Ephraim R. McLean 3rd, *A Computer-Based Medical History System: Factors Affecting Its Acceptance and Use by Physicians* (unpublished Ph.D. thesis), Sloan School of Management, M.I.T., January 1970.

[34] J. Grossman, G. O. Barnett, D. Smedlow, and M. McGuire, "The Collection of Medical History Data Using a Real-Time Computer System," *Proceedings of the Annual Conference on Engineering in Medicine and Biology,* Houston, Tex., 1968.

[35] "Report of Activities of Laboratory of Computer Science," 1968, pp. 1–2. Bolt Beranek & Newman Inc. is no longer involved with these activities, which have developed into a series of several smaller, better-focused research studies. Dr. Barnett observes:
We have abandoned the "total systems" approach to the development of a

Laboratory, with direct reporting of test results to the emergency ward and intensive care units. A later stage of the project will provide for direct connection to the automated instrumentation in the Chemistry Laboratory, and eventually extension of the computer-aided reporting system to the other 32 laboratories in the hospital. Later on, the system can be transferred to other medical centers for use in their laboratories.

• A laboratory data-transmission system has been developed at the University of Missouri Medical Center. The computer collects data from six laboratories, prints out results and evaluations, including additional interpretations that may establish new laboratory determination interrelationships.[36]

• A Clinical Decision Support System, developed at IBM, has been used experimentally to provide doctors in their offices and in hospitals with "the latest information about ailments and their remedies." Using a keyboard and display screen in a portable terminal, a doctor can get the latest information available as an aid to his diagnosis.[37]

• A medical information network for hospitals is the objective of Medinet, a General Electric subsidiary centered in the Boston area. By early 1969, this system was being tested in a number of hospitals in New England, and was actually in use in one hospital in New York State.

• The National Library of Medicine in Bethesda, Maryland, has been perfecting its MEDLARS (Medical Literature Analysis and Retrieval System), developed initially in 1963. Its intention was to produce a monthly

---

hospital information system in favor of a modular evolutionary activity, wherein we proceed in a type of hill-climbing fashion, developing and implementing relatively separate subsystems. We feel that this is a much more productive approach and that integration of the subsystems will be relatively simple compared to the task of the development of each subsystem. P. 1.

[36] For a full account of this system, see Donald A. B. Lindberg, *The Computer and Medical Care,* Springfield, Ill.: Charles C Thomas, Publishers, 1968, pp. 67–77. Dr. Lindberg is Director of the Medical Center Computer Program at the University of Missouri.

[37] *The New York Times,* September 25, 1967; see also *Datamation,* vol. 11, no. 12, December 1965, p. 28.

computerized list of some 14,000 articles in the biomedical field, but delays were reported by physicians in utilizing it effectively.[38]

• A proposed national computer-based medical record system has been discussed in Great Britain, which has a national health service;[39] and the Food and Drug Administration in the United States claims to have put a major computer system in operation to give all its experts in field offices better access to the agency's technical data. It would provide instant data on new drugs under investigation and would monitor abuses of narcotics and psychedelic drug compounds.[40]

Planning and Managing Complex Medical and Surgical Procedures

Using Critical Path and PERT methods taken from computer applications in industry, a team of doctors have planned and carried out kidney transplant operations through a number of computer runs.[41] Simulation of procedures in advance of the actual surgical operation would seem to be a logical application of computer-based systems, but published reports on further applications are lacking.

Hospital Administration

In addition to accounting, payrolls, patient billing, dietary administration, and menu planning (all noted earlier), some recent applications have involved various forms of "inventory control" such as

• Assuring full bed occupancy, by careful patient scheduling, as has been done at the Massachusetts Eye and Ear Infirmary.

[38] *Hospital Physician,* vol. 2, no. 9, September 1966, p. 48. See also *The New York Times,* February 6, 1966, and *Guide to Medlars Services,* National Library of Medicine, Section F, p. 1, U.S. Department of Health, Education and Welfare, November 1966.

[39] "U.K. Council Proposes Medical Data Bank," *Datamation,* vol. 13, no. 9, September 1967, p. 105.

[40] "Drug Computer to Expand Data," *The New York Times,* August 12, 1967, p. 11; also *Business Week,* no. 1981, August 19, 1967, p. 60.

[41] "Planning and Managing Complex Medical and Surgical Procedures," in special issue on computers, *Journal of the American Medical Association,* vol. 196, no. 11, June 13, 1966.

• Control of blood bank supplies, to assure use in the right order to prevent spoilage and losses.[42]

• The Children's Hospital Medical Center in Boston has a fully operative on-line real-time system for patient location control, utilizing a patient admitting information system in connection with a bed location system.[43]

Medical Education

As computer experiments and applications in medical and hospital services are spreading, it is natural that they should be introduced in medical education. Some examples are the following:

• Fourth-year medical students at the University of California at Los Angeles are given computer presentations of hypothetical patient medical histories and tests that they then diagnose and recommend treatment. The computer program checks the validity of their work. This is claimed to be superior to clinical experience, in which the student finds diagnosis and treatment developed by the staff, with little opportunity for his own separate diagnosis.[44]

• A computer-controlled patient simulator has been developed at the Medical School of the University of Southern California to train resident physicians in anesthesiology.[45]

• The Laboratory of Computer Science of the Department of Medicine at the Massachusetts General Hospital has engaged in a number of teaching efforts, including a "medical student medical record," which uses a medical summary completed by each student on his cases

---

[42] This was Lockheed Aircraft's first venture into computerized hospital systems. *Fortune,* vol. LXXV, no. 1, January 1967, p. 186. Lockheed was also developing a computer center or utility for 58 San Francisco Bay hospitals.

[43] L. W. Cronkhite, Jr., "Patient Location Control as a First Step Toward a Total Information System," *Hospitals,* vol. 41, no. 9, May 1, 1967, pp. 107–112.

[44] *The New York Times,* February 2, 1968.

[45] *Datamation,* vol. 13, no. 5, May 1967, p. 77. For further details on this simulator and other aspects of computers in medical education, see *Proceedings of the Conference on the Use of Computers in Medical Education,* April 3, 4, and 5, 1968, University of Oklahoma, Oklahoma City, Okla.

in the clinics, to report both to the students and the faculty a summary "so that they can have a better understanding of the type and character of the treatment they give."[46] A lecture-laboratory course in computer science is also offered to clinical and research fellows of the hospital. Some Harvard Medical School students are employed part-time in the Laboratory of Computer Science.

Some Long-Run Implications of Computer Applications

1. There will be further reduction of routine, time-consuming work by professionals and subprofessionals. If it is remotely true, as one computer specialist has claimed, that 90 percent of the physician's time is spent in information gathering for patient diagnosis and treatment, then this "is the kind of task that can be programmed into a computer."[47] As the Surgeon General of the U.S. Public Health Service has put it: "The challenge to the physician is to use computers to help do the burdensome part of the medical workup, so that he may give his full attention to the creative, human part."[48]

2. The shortages of professionals and subprofessionals in this field should be somewhat relieved by computer programs that handle the routine tasks reviewed in the preceding sections. But the more complex systems in which computer technology is involved initially require more medical and paramedical personnel. Furthermore, with the expanding demand for medical and hospital care, it seems unlikely that there will be any eventual displacement of personnel. Their professional talents will certainly be better utilized, and some expansion of services should be possible with a higher ratio of patients to physicians. Computerization of patient's medical histories, preliminary assignments to specialists, preliminary diagnosis, and easy

[46] G. Octo Barnett, 1968 Report, pp. 7–8, as cited in ftn. 35.

[47] Evon C. Greanias, "The Computer in Medicine," *Datamation,* vol. 11, no. 12, December 1965, p. 28.

[48] Dr. William H. Stewart, *Datamation,* vol. 14, no. 1, January 1968, p. 57.

access to medical records from the data bank should be a boon, rather than a threat, to busy physicians.[49]

However, this means that *some* present work of physicians will be taken over by computers and by nonphysician clerical practitioners.[50] Those who now fail to keep up-to-date on recent developments may be able to do so with information-retrieval systems similar to Medlars. Computers may, therefore, even help some to become better physicians.[51]

3. The view that physicians will not be displaced, even though the nature of their work may be changed, is challenged by a prediction that the computer and other highly specialized equipment will be operated by an army of technicians, who will routinely hook up the patients and maintain the equipment.[52] The large number of physicians, as we know them, will dwindle into a small cadre of medical scholars. The authors also point out that no matter how many physicians and related personnel are trained, "we cannot keep up with the demand for health services. Technologists, technicians and aides in the patient-care spectrum are means to extend the productivity of the physician—the human computer." They add that the human computer has certain weaknesses—failing hearing and vision, as well as personal worries that distort perception—while the computer itself is "always available."

[49] M. S. Blumberg, "Computers Will Augment Physician's Role," *Modern Hospital*, vol. 106, no. 48, 1966.

[50] This point has been made in a significant review of recent developments by G. Octo Barnett and Anthony Robbins, "Information Technology and Manpower Productivity," *Journal of the American Medical Association*, vol. 209, no. 4, July 28, 1969. Pp. 546–548.

[51] This is the view of Dr. Donald A. B. Lindberg, *The Computer and Medical Care*, Springfield, Ill.. Charles C Thomas, Publishers, 1968. Dr. Lindberg believes that "new information-science techniques offer the first possibility of reversing this trend (toward medical specialities) by making a very large corpus of knowledge available to each physician through automatic means. . . . The individual physician of the future should be able to draw information and guidance for treatment from many specialty areas without attempting to read the literature of many specialities at once." Pp. 179–180.

[52] Edmund J. McTernan (Dean of Health Sciences at Northeastern University) and Dr. Dean Crocker (of Children's Hospital), writing in the *Hospital Physician*, and quoted in "The Computerized Hospital of the Future Is Visualized," *The Boston Herald-Traveler*, March 23, 1969.

The official American Medical Association view is clearly at variance with the foregoing prediction:

If one general conclusion is possible, it is the statement that no computer will attain an MD degree, nor replace a single physician. The computer can be an extraordinarily useful aid, and we should become better acquainted with the potentialities and limitations of these electronic devices. But despite the theories of certain enthusiasts, the computer cannot offset any present or future shortage of physicians. A current relevant quip states: "Any doctor who *can* be replaced by a machine, *deserves* to be replaced by a machine."[53]

4. The future possibilities of man-machine interaction in medical and hospital services are impressive. The sequential diagnosis experiment being developed by Professor Gorry and Dr. Barnett at the Massachusetts General Hospital, as reviewed earlier, is an illustration of an interactive system between the doctor and the computer, designed eventually to assist the doctor in his diagnosis in real time. So is the electrocardiographic analysis provided by the Mt. Sinai Medical Center in New York for physicians in West Virginia hospitals. The availability of patient's medical records from a computer data bank is less interactive, as is any other form of information retrieval from stored sources. But all of these are computer-aids to decision making and represent a true man-machine partnership, as a 1966 article in the *Hospital Physician* noted:

For most M.D.'s in computer projects the supreme goal is to help the physician in his management of patients. They don't want or expect the computer to tell the doctor what to do, but they believe it can mark out guidelines and perform specific services that will directly aid his decision making.[54]

The same observations may be made about interactive computer systems that can assist nurses, technicians,

---

[53] Editorial in *Journal of the American Medical Association* (special issue on computers), vol. 196, no. 11, June 13, 1966, p. 1015.

[54] Lead paragraph in "The Computer and Its Effect on Hospital Physicians—Guiding Diagnosis and Treatment," *Hospital Physician,* vol. 2, no. 9, September 1966, p. 47.

dieticians, and office staff in hospitals, as they make decisions and perform their assigned tasks.

5. Some centralization of organization structures is likely to occur as computer centers in large hospitals or computer service centers serving groups of hospitals replace some of the clerical functions that each participating hospital previously performed. Examples are accounting, billing, payrolls, and medical records. Possibly the remaining hospital clerical staffs will perform somewhat different functions: providing computer inputs and analyzing computer outputs, rather than keeping and retrieving records directly. Area-wide or regional medical records will require better interhospital cooperation. Centralization of computer services will make available certain specialized functions more widely (such as computer analysis of electrocardiograms), and in one sense, may strengthen decentralized units in the hospital system of the country.

6. All of these developments may herald "The Coming Revolution in Medicine," to borrow the title of a recent book by Dr. David D. Rutstein, Head of the Department of Preventive Medicine at the Harvard Medical School. Arguing for a complete reorganization of the delivery of medical care, Dr. Rutstein believes that computers will act as information clearing houses to aid physicians in the diagnosis of disease as well as processing laboratory tests and assisting in medical research. He also foresees a reallocation of physician's duties, some delegated to trained technicians, some performed by machines—leaving the physician to spend his time on problems that demand his special education, training, and talents.[55] This is termed "a more radical potential for technological applications as a result of the thrust toward changes in the use of manpower in the organization of health care delivery."[56]

[55] David D. Rutstein, *The Coming Revolution in Medicine,* Cambridge, Mass.: The M.I.T. Press, 1968.

[56] G. Octo Barnett and Anthony Robbins, "Information Technology and Manpower Productivity," *Journal of the American Medical Association,* vol. 209, no. 4, July 28, 1969, p. 547.

Resistances to Be Met and Overcome

The exciting possibilities of computer applications to meet some of the needs outlined at the beginning of this chapter will not be widely realized until doctors, subprofessionals and others in hospitals and medical care understand how these can help them in their work. The conservatism of the medical profession is well known, and as one doctor active in computer programs has noted, this is "another factor which has limited the iniitiative of hospitals in the dynamic application of computer techniques to the area of patient care."[57]

If the lessons from both unsuccessful and successful computer applications can be summarized, they suggest the following steps are necessary for forward progress:

1. Initial commitment on the part of the hospital administration that experimentation and eventual implementation are necessary.

2. Direct involvement of the medical and nursing staff, as well as other specialized groups, in developing, testing, and implementing subsystems in particular parts or functions of the hospital. Some of these should be encouraged by hospital management to volunteer for (or be assigned to) these projects.

3. Avoidance of what someone has called "a priesthood of programmers," through which all changes in information handling must go, is imperative. The same comment could be made about system designers who fail to consult practicing physicians. One physician reported participating in "a simple compilation regarding one disease," for which over 10,000 questionnaires covering about 20 questions were gathered and turned over to trained programmers who were not, however, physicians. The results were useless, and the study had to be reprogrammed after physicians had rephrased the questions and methods of approach.[58] The full facts in this case are not reported, so

[57] *Report to the Computer Research Study Section,* National Institutes of Health, p. 33.
[58] Dr. Irving S. Wright, Professor of Medicine at Cornell Medical

it is possible that, until the error occurred, physicians may have abrogated their responsibility to become involved in the program from its inception.

4. Continuing involvement of hospital or medical center management is vital in selecting objectives, determining priorities in areas for study of computer applications, and subsequent support and help as problems are encountered.[59]

5. Finally, an evolutionary approach is desirable, because the profession changes slowly and successful applications depend on full understanding and appreciation of the ways in which computer-based systems can aid doctors and hospital staffs rather than threaten them.

Summary

The spread of actual and experimental computer applications in medical and hospital services may be summarized in the following points:

1. Shortages of medical and hospital personnel have been acerbated by the information explosion in this knowledge-based field, as in the ones reviewed earlier. The possibility of errors and the need to provide rapid information-processing assistance to harried hospital staffs explain much of the growing interest in computer applications.

2. Hospital administration, processing of medical records and histories, and electrocardiogram analysis have been the principal areas in which computers have been used. Other computer-based information gathering and retrieval systems are spreading. Computer-aided diagnosis is still largely in the experimental stage, but future possibilities could be the most significant of any.

3. Computers have reduced some of the routine and time-consuming work previously performed by clerical,

College, in his presidential address before the American College of Physicians, San Francisco, April 10, 1967, as reported in *The New York Times,* April 11, 1967.

[59] "...innovations that use computer technology are most successful and best accepted when there is cooperation between computernicks and health care experts, with clearly identified needs and well-defined objectives." G. Octo Barnett, "The Computer's Role in Health-Service Research," *Technology Review,* vol. 72, no. 6, April 1970, p. 58.

subprofessional, and even professional people in medical
and hospital services; this will undoubtedly spread further.
Shortages of skilled and professional people may be relieved
somewhat, but the development of advanced computer
systems, especially in information gathering and retrieval
and in computer-aided diagnosis, requires new kinds of
scarce personnel such as systems designers and
programmers.

4. Man-machine systems will spread faster in
hospitals, clinics, and group medical practice than in
private practice by individual physicians. But even private
doctors will be able to practice more effectively with the
assistance of medical information retrieval systems,
electrocardiogram analysis, and eventually computer-aided
diagnosis.

5. The speed with which computer-based systems spread
in hospitals and medical practice will depend in part on
the methods of introduction. If systems designers work with
hospital personnel and with doctors (especially in group
practice) in the development of systems that have to be
understood to be used, then resistance will be reduced and
acceptance hastened.

5. National and Centralized Local Data Banks

We have seen that some local data banks have been used
for crime prevention and law enforcement, and that one
national data bank developed by the F.B.I. has been used
for this purpose. In this chapter we shall examine the use
of national and centralized local data banks for research
and administrative purposes. At the national level, the
emphasis has been on research for its own sake and for
improving policy formulation. At the local level, the
programs have been designed to assist local and county
governments in more effective planning and administration
of government services. There has been little controversy
over the local data banks, but the national proposal has
raised such a storm of protest that it has not yet been
implemented. The history of this abortive effort is
instructive on the problems of developing highly
centralized data banks that raise the question of individual
privacy of information contained therein.

The Proposed National Data Center

The discussion of this proposal has involved high-level
committees, two congressional hearings, and numerous
supporters and critics. At this writing, there is no
comprehensive National Data Center, despite the
committee's recommendations. But there are several partial
national data banks in a number of federal agencies in the
Departments of Agriculture, Labor, Interior, Commerce,
Treasury, and Health, Education and Welfare, as well as
in the Board of Governors of the Federal Reserve System.[1]

The Needs

The necessity for a National Data Center was developed in
two outstanding committees, supported by a report of the
Joint Economic Committee of the Congress, and
subsequently by a committee of the Division of Behavioral
Sciences of the National Research Council.[2] The needs that

---

[1] As noted in the Report of the Committee on the Preservation and Use
Use of Economic Data, to the Social Science Research Council,
Washington, D.C., April 1965. This is known as the Ruggles Report,
named for its Chairman, Professor Richard Ruggles of the Department of
Economics, Yale University.

[2] This section draws material from Robert L. Chartrand, "The Federal

such a center would fulfill may be summarized in the following points:

1. The present organization of federal statistical information, much of it on machine-readable tapes, does not lend itself to optimal use of these vast amounts of data for economic research and analysis. (The Ruggles Report.)

2. There is need for a "large scale systematic demographic, economic and social statistics file" the purpose of which is "the assembly of statistical frequency distributions of the many characteristics which groups of individuals (or households, business enterprises or other reporting units) share." (Testimony of Professor Carl Kaysen at Senate Subcommittee Hearings; Kaysen was chairman of a Task Force on the Storage of and Access to Government Statistics, reporting to the Director of the Bureau of the Budget.)

3. "The data center would supply to all users, inside and outside the Government, frequency distributions, summaries, analyses, but never data on individuals or other single reporting units. The technology of machine storage and processing would make it possible for these outputs to be tailored closely to the needs of individual users without great expense and without disclosure of individual data. This is just what is not possible under our decentralized system." (Kaysen testimony.)

4. The center would include existing bodies of data already collected by such federal agencies as the Census, the Bureau of Labor Statistics, the National Center for Health Statistics, the Office of Education, the Department of Agriculture, and the Department of Commerce. Additional data generated as a result of the administration of the federal income tax and the federal social security systems would be included. But the Kaysen Committee

Data Center: Proposals and Reactions," Legislative Reference Service, Library of Congress, Washington, D.C., June 14, 1965; and from testimony and appendixes in the hearings on "Computers and Invasion of Privacy," before the Special Subcommittee on Invasion of Privacy, of the House Committee on Government Operations, July 26, 27, 28, 1966, and "Computer Privacy," Hearings before the Subcommittee on Administrative Practice and Procedure of the Senate Committee on the Judiciary, March 14 and 15, 1967, and February 8, 1968.

specifically excluded police dossiers from the F.B.I., Civil
Service personnel records, personnel data on the armed
services, or any other personal information. While no one,
through the Center, could find out an individual's income
or tax paid, knowledge of aggregates of income, by sources,
would be useful to the Congress and to the Executive
branch in generating tax policy.

5. "The central problem of data use is one of associating
numerical records and the greatest efficiency of the existing
Federal statistical system is its failure to provide access to
data in a way that permits the association of the elements
of data sets in order to identify and measure the
interrelationship among interdependent or related
observations. This is true at virtually all levels of use and
for all purposes from academic model builders to business
market researchers." (Edgar S. Dunn, Jr., of Resources for
the Future, Inc., in his evaluation report of the Ruggles
Report, made at the request of the Bureau of the Budget,
November 1, 1965.)[3]

6. Better coordination and integration of separate
government statistical programs is essential, and it was the
view of the Joint Economic Committee that the current
statistical information is "totally inadequate to meet the
changing policy needs of our times."[4]

7. The information explosion requires that behavioral and
social scientists develop computerized information systems
before the flow of research data rises "to blood heights."
This was the view expressed in a committee report of the
Division of Behavioral Sciences of the National Research
Council, which is the operating agency of the National
Academy of Sciences.[5] The report recommended a
decentralized national network of data banks containing

[3] This report, as well as the full Ruggles Report, is found in the
Appendix to the House Subcommittee Hearings on "The Computer and
the Invasion of Privacy." The Dunn quotation is on p. 255.

[4] *The Coordination and Integration of Government Statistical Programs,*
Subcommittee on Economic Statistics, Joint Economic Committee, U.S.
Congress, Washington: U.S. Government Printing Office, 1967, p. 4.

[5] *Communication Systems and Resources in the Behavioral Sciences,* summarized
in *The New York Times,* January 14, 1967.

statistical information, and a federal data center to coordinate the government's statistical output.

The Problem of Privacy

Will a proposed National Data Center expose individuals to loss of privacy and maybe blackmail by those who gain access to an individual's records? This concern has monopolized the two congressional hearings, and even the experts are divided on the issue. The same problem applies to the limited national computerized data banks in present federal agencies, as well as to the county and city data banks, which will be discussed later.

The Critics

An editorial in *The New York Times* in 1966 put the fears of a National Data Center in these words:

Can personal privacy survive the ceaseless advances of the technological juggernaut? ... The Orwellian nightmare would be brought very close indeed if Congress permits the proposed computer National Data Center to come into being. We already live with the fact that from birth to the grave Federal agencies keep tabs on each of us, recording our individual puny existence, monitoring our incomes and claimed deductions, noting when we are employed or jobless, and—through the F.B.I. and similar agencies—keeping all too close watch on what we say, what we read and what organizations we belong to.... What is now proposed is the amalgamation of these files, and the creation of a situation in which the push of a button would promptly dredge up all that is known about anyone. Understandably, this idea has brought vigorous protest, in which we join. Aside from the opportunities for blackmail and from the likelihood that the record of any single past transgression might damage one for life, this proposed device would approach the effective end of privacy....[6]

Vance Packard, the best-seller author who has written on the erosion of privacy in his book, *The Naked Society,* has testified before the Gallagher Subcommittee of the House of Representatives in the same vein, and has criticized the proposed National Data Center for four reasons: (1) it "threatens to encourage a depersonalization of the

---

[6] *The New York Times,* August 9, 1966. It is clear that the editorial writer was not aware of the more limited proposals summarized in the preceding section.

American way of life," (2) it "is likely to increase the distrust of citizens in their own government and alienate them from it," (3) "a central file can absorb large batches of data about people but is ill-equipped to correct errors, allow for extenuating circumstances, or bring facts up to date," and (4) it would place "so much power in the hands of the people in a position of power to push computer buttons." He adds:

When the details of our lives are fed into a central computer or other vast file-keeping system, we all fall under the control of the machine's managers to some extent..... My own hunch is that Big Brother, if he comes to the United States, will turn out to be not a greedy power-seeker but a relentless bureaucrat obsessed with efficiency. And he, more than the single power-seeker, could lead us to that ultimate of horrors, a humanity in chains of plastic tape.[7]

The public statements of Representative Gallagher and Senator Long, during or following the hearings they conducted, are not dissimilar from these views. Indeed, Packard quotes extensively from Representative Gallagher.

The critics from the universities are mostly law professors, prominent among whom is Alan F. Westin, Professor of Public Law at Columbia University and author of a book, *Privacy and Freedom*.[8] In his testimony before the Long subcommittee in the Senate, Westin expressed the view that the proposed National Data Center

would clearly lack the careful development, the system safeguards, the administrative procedures, and certainly the type of legal framework that would be necessary to protect individuals and groups if information from many Federal agencies were to be collected, stored, and used in unspecified ways, thus raising the very problems of the incorporation of data collections that you mentioned in your opening statement.[9]

Senator Long had expressed fear that the proposed National Data "Bank" is "designed to store names and

---

[7] Vance Packard, "Don't Tell It to the Computer," *New York Times Magazine,* January 8, 1967, pp. 44–45ff. The quotation is on pp. 90–92.

[8] Alan F. Westin, *Privacy and Freedom,* New York: Atheneum Publishers, 1967.

[9] Long subcommittee hearings, Senate, p. 282.

information on citizens so that the simple push of a button will spread a citizen's life history on the computer readout."[10]

In a more recent statement, Professor Westin has suggested that proper safeguards in computerized data banks should include the following: (1) privacy—whether certain kinds of information should be collected at all in these systems, the extent to which one piece of information should be disclosed and circulated and to whom; (2) due process—giving an individual the opportunity to know what is in his data file, to challenge its accuracy, and to contest interpretations based on the facts; and (3) public audit and review, in the form of a watchdog or ombudsman-type agency, or legislative agencies, or public review boards, and so forth. Westin believes that public concern over the issue is forcing public and private organizations to become more self-conscious about the role of privacy and the role of information in our society; and this exercise could—if properly nurtured and protected— lead us to give more protection to individual rights than we provided in the pre-computer era.[11]

---

[10] "Opening Statement of Senator Long," p. 276. I leave it to the reader's recollection whether *this* is what the supporters of the Center proposed.

[11] Alan F. Westin, "Computers and the Protection of Privacy," *The Technology Review*, vol. 7, no. 6, April 1969, pp. 32–37. Westin's views are apparently shared by Professor Robert M. Fano, who was the first director of Project MAC at M.I.T. In a recent unpublished paper he noted that the Compatible Time Sharing System at M.I.T. "is far from adequate in its protection of privacy." Although every user has his own password, he can give this to other users "or to everybody." Furthermore, " systems programmers are fallible, and mistakes in the control programs of the system may remain undetected for a long time. As a matter of fact, they may be discovered by users inclined to exploit them for their own advantage or for other malicious purposes. Our experience at M.I.T. indicates that these dangers are very real and that no community can be assumed to be immune from them.... There is no simple answer to the problem of protecting a computer system against intruders. ....The right to privacy must be defined and protected by suitable legislation, and also appropriate regulations must be enacted to protect the users of public computer systems." R. M. Fano, "Implications of Computers for Society," paper presented at the Joint Summer Conference on "The Computer in the University," Technical University of Berlin and Massachusetts Institute of Technology, Berlin, Federal Republic of Germany, July 22–August 2, 1968, p. 8.

The Defenders and Their Proposals for Protecting Privacy
Most of those who favored the National Data Center for
statistical purposes argued that individual economic and
social data should not be revealed, and that the data bank
would *not* contain detailed personal dossiers about
individuals and life histories. Many of these explanations
were offered at the congressional hearings, frequently in
answer to queries from the subcommittee chairmen or their
staffs. However persuasive they might be to an objective
reader of the testimony, they did not convince the
congressional subcommittees.

After denying that the proposed center would contain any
individual dossier with personal data of any kind, Kaysen
subsequently tried to suggest the following safeguard on
revealing other individual data (such as incomes, job
experience, mobility, and so on):

Everytime anyone calls out a file or a group of files out of
the Data Center, he has to make a record entry that says,
"I am so and so, I have called out files number so and so,
and so and so, and I have called them out pursuant to
such and such a job order." Thus, he leaves a trail, and
the machine, and the programs which operate it, can be so
organized that nobody can operate the machine without
leaving a trail, unless he tries to eradicate both the trail
and the data in the machine and thus shows to his
supervisors that something has gone wrong.[12]

Kaysen has also pointed out that the distinction between a
personal dossier and the assembly of statistical frequency
distributions based on individual economic and social data
is not self-applying, and "administrators and bureaucrats,
checked and overseen by politicians, have to apply it. But
so it is ever."[13]

The same point was made at the Long subcommittee
hearings by Dr. E. R. Piore, Chief Scientist of IBM, who
after describing the Project MAC system of protection of

[12] Long subcommittee hearings, p. 9. Despite this, Senator Long at a
later point, questioning another witness, said "If we did go on this cradle-
to-the-grave deal, everything in regard to that individual would be
collected and by pushing a button you could get all of the information (on
the individual) if it was put in a machine like that." P. 116.

[13] Carl Kaysen, "Data Banks and Dossiers," *The Public Interest,* Spring
1967 (reproduced in Long subcommittee hearings, pp. 265–269).

access at M.I.T., and in-company management information systems concluded:

...preservation of privacy rests not with machines but with men. The effectiveness of all protective measures, however sophisticated they may become, will still depend upon people; operators, service personnel, supervising officers, and all those who decide what information to put into a computer and how to use it.... Machines have no morals, no ethics: men have ethics and morals.[14]

The present confidentiality of individual data in Census reports, protected by law and by administrative action, has been cited as a good example of the protection of privacy which could equally well be applied to the proposed National Data Center. As Kaysen pointed out:

The present law and practice governing the Census Bureau offer a model for this purpose. The law provides that information contained in an individual Census return may not be disclosed either to the general public or to other agencies of the government, nor may such information be used for law-enforcement, regulatory, or tax-collection activity in respect to any individual respondent. This statutory restriction has been effectively enforced, and the Census Bureau has maintained for years the confidence of respondents in its will and ability to protect the information they give to it. The same statutory restraints could and should be extended to the data center, and the same results could be expected of it.[15]

Despite the answers of the proponents, those who feared the advent of an Orwellian 1984 "Big Brother," in the form of a computer whose "button could be pushed" to print out revealing and damaging information about an individual, carried the day. The proposal for a National Data Center is in limbo, even though there are a number of national subsystems in different federal agencies. The benefits that might derive from statistical analysis of aggregates based on individual economic and social data are casualties of the fear that individual privacy might be eroded. Even the sensible proposals of Alan Westin, reviewed earlier, have not received serious discussion in the

[14] Long subcommittee hearings, pp. 122–123.

[15] Kaysen, "Data Banks and Dossiers" (p. 268 in Long subcommittee hearings).

congressional subcommittees that killed the national data bank proposal.

Local Data Banks

As Westin pointed out in his congressional testimony, there seems to have been little concern about the privacy question in the efforts to develop local data banks. These have been developed in such cities as New Haven and Detroit, or in Alameda County, California. A brief review of each of these will indicate their purposes, recent status, and relation to the privacy issue.

1. The City of New Haven, with the help of IBM's Advanced Systems Development Division, began in 1967 to "put the city's files on computers to obtain a statistical profile of everyone in town. . . . The knowledge, for example, that a man was crippled could be stored away for possible use by the Fire Department. His application for welfare assistance could be automatically checked to see if he owned a car. . . . The police chief could have instant access to all the information about a suspect, [and] the computer system could also determine if a fire broke out near a convicted arsonist's home."[16] This type of data bank, unlike the proposed national one, apparently does have individual dossiers, with cross-referencing.

2. Detroit has been developing two data banks, one containing physical data and the other social data. "The physical data bank contains such information as the condition of the city's residential, commercial, and industrial housing, obsolescent structures, crime rates, and much more" to help plan urban renewal projects. The social data bank "includes statistics on crime rates, welfare, births and deaths, school truancy and drop out rates, the occurence of venereal diseases and tuberculosis, and other information." Printouts of social data are made quarterly and can be retrieved by census tracts when needed. Apparently, social data are used in urban planning, also, for the statement is made that "we cannot improve a

[16] "New Haven Plans a Computer Pool," *The New York Times,* March 29, 1967.

neighborhood's social vitality if we do not know what the neighborhood's social problems are and how its people live." Also, "in time we may even be able to devise an 'early warning system,' which could alert us to a neighborhood drifting into instability or social decline."[17] There is no mention of the possibility that individual data may be revealed.

3. The Alameda County "People Information System" includes the City of Oakland, California, and surrounding area with a population over 1 million.[18] The system consists of two parallel but separate real-time subsystems: (1) a central index for social services "to better coordinate the line activities of the social service agencies like welfare, hospitals, health, and probation," and (2) a police information network. Both subsystems have data on individuals, since the first can "identify people, locate their records, and thus respond to the thousands of inquiries pouring in each day by telephone, by letter, and by walk-ins." The second real-time subsystem, known as PIN, contains warrants of arrests "to serve the 93 law enforcement agencies in the Greater San Francisco Bay Area." The benefits claimed are "more efficient government" (particularly in preparing reports to different state departments) and "increased service" in better law enforcement, better future planning, and in "helping welfare, health and probation social workers spot and control potential trouble areas before—not after—the fact." The privacy question is skirted with the note that "most information handled by counties is of a nonconfidential nature and security requirements are not involved." But for files that are confidential, "access is carefully controlled by permitting only authorized terminals, and where necessary authorized persons—by means of secret codes—to inquire into such files. Future plans also call for

---

[17] Harold Black and Edward Shaw, "Detroit's Data Banks," *Datamation*, vol. 13, no. 3, March 1967, pp. 26–27. The authors are staff members of the city's Community Renewal Program.

[18] Gordon Milliman, "Alameda County's 'People Information System,' " *Datamation*, vol. 13, no. 3, March 1967, pp. 28–31.

monitoring techniques to determine what terminals are accessing any given file."

Summary: Some Implications of Centralized Data Banks

Some implications drawn from the preceding discussion may be summarized in the following points:

1. The proposal for a National Data Center was designed primarily to permit large-scale statistical analysis of the characteristics of groups of individuals, households, or business establishments. The purpose was to aid in policy planning at the national level. In contrast, the local and regional data banks have been designed and used primarily for administrative purposes.

2. Despite the limited objectives of the National Data Center proposal, the issue of "privacy" if individual data or "dossiers" was raised by congressional committees and a number of critics of the proposal. The objectives of the proposal were distorted by some of these critics, who suggested that a "1984-Big Brother" type of surveillance of all that any individual ever did in his lifetime would be available in a computer printout "at the touch of a button." These distortions, along with some more moderate criticism, resulted in the indefinite postponement of any national data bank.

3. The issue of privacy of computer-based information is, nonetheless, a real one. A number of useful suggestions have been made to protect access to data on individuals, and these would require both legislative and administrative controls. Presumably, these could be made effective, in order that the legitimate research objectives of a national data bank could be realized.

4. In contrast, the issue of privacy has not been raised about the local and regional data banks, which admittedly do contain detailed information about individuals. Municipal governments have apparently been less concerned about possible misuse of such data than was the Congress about a national data bank.

5. Unlike the other "knowledge industries" reviewed earlier in this volume, there do not seem to be important

organizational implications about these data banks. The
proposed national center would not lead to more
centralization of government as such but to more
centralization of final statistical collection and analysis.
There is no published evidence that the few local and
regional centralized data banks have led to greater
centralization of governmental administration.

6. Implementation of centralized data banks has not
threatened the jobs of existing governmental personnel; nor
has it drastically changed the nature of their jobs. The
main obstacle in implementing the National Data Center
has been the privacy question. Quite possibly, greater
attention to ways of protecting individual privacy in the
earlier special committee reports that recommended such a
center would have forestalled some of the opposition. But
in retrospect it is not at all certain that *any* such
recommendations would have prevented the raising of a
politically attractive and often emotional issue. Perhaps
only time and patience will overcome this obstacle.

6. Summary and Conclusions

As the computer has spread in the management of enterprises, its special advantages have also been apparent to those concerned with developing more effective services in other fields. This study has concentrated on some of the knowledge-based fields in which the growth of information has been rapid, shortages of trained and professional personnel have limited the effectiveness of services offered, and man-machine possibilities have, therefore, seemed important to expand.

While many fields of human endeavor can be considered "knowledge-based," the analysis presented in the preceding chapters has been confined to five principal areas: (1) formal education, including the administration of educational institutions; (2) library systems and subsystems; (3) legal and legislative services, administration of justice, and crime prevention and law enforcement; (4) medical and hospital services; and (5) national and centralized local data banks for research and administrative uses. The literature on computer applications in each of these fields is voluminous and growing, and no one can pretend to cover every development. This review has been selective but representative of initial and recent developments in each field covered.

In considering reported introductions in computer-based systems, it is important to distinguish between the present reality and the future possibilities. In some cases information on this distinction is not easily available. Wherever possible, the differences between actual systems now in use, those still in the experimental stage, and those further in the future have been indicated at various points in the preceding chapters. One conclusion clearly emerges from this analysis: proponents of specific computer-based systems tend to be more optimistic about their rapid spread and acceptance than subsequent experience has borne out. In some cases, they are more visionary than realistic about the possibilities in the near future, measured in terms of a decade.

Administrators and professionals in these knowledge-based

fields ignore even the visionaries at their peril, however. What seems unlikely tomorrow will be reality some years from now. Implications of the spread of the computer need to be considered now. More specifically, consideration should be given to the needs that have encouraged and will require the use of computer-based systems, the effect of these systems on the ways in which work is and will be performed in the organization, the impact on organization structures, the possible resistances of people to the new systems, and ways in which these may be reduced to achieve effective man-machine relationships. Actual displacement of specialized and professional people may be limited because of present shortages in these knowledge-based fields. But foot-dragging occurs because people fear the unknown, or because they have lacked involvement in the development of new systems.

Summary by Fields

With these general points in mind, the following is a brief summary of the principal developments and implications in each of the five knowledge-based fields covered in this study.

1. Formal Education and Educational Administration

The needs that computers have or might serve here are in relieving teachers of repetitive drill-type work; providing them with continuous evaluation of computer-stored student records; permitting slower students to set their own pace in computer-aided instruction as well as enabling faster or advanced students to use the computer for more difficult work; improving instruction in basic structured subjects; enabling students to understand and work with the computer itself; and assisting educational administrators in allocating more effectively the total resources available to them.

There have been developments to meet each of these needs, some more successful than others. Computer-aided instruction seems to have developed faster in elementary and secondary education, although much of what is reported is still in the pilot-project or experimental stage.

No large public school system is using computer-aided instruction in all of the teaching programs where it might be applicable. In higher education, some experiments are under way in computer-aided instruction, but the most widespread impact is in the use of in-house computers for computational purposes by an increasing proportion of college and university students. A number of universities are using computers in the administration of educational services and in achieving better allocation of educational resources.

It seems likely that in the long run computers will become widespread in formal education, particularly in the repetitive and structured type of subject matter. Costs will have to come down substantially, and school districts will have to commit proportionately more of their resources to this type of expenditure or receive subsidies to permit wider use of computer-aided instruction. When either of these occurs, the role of the teacher may be changed from that of one who conveys structured information to one who helps students with difficult nonstructured questions. There will be more opportunity for teachers to innovate, as members of a team of educational specialists. Smaller schools may buy packaged programs from educational utilities, and some schools and colleges will become the educational developers of computer-aided instruction systems. Possibly the "learning corporations" (book publishers merged with computer companies) will also develop such systems, but their record to date has fallen short of earlier expectations.

If computer-aided instruction is to spread with the support of teachers and the educational establishment, efforts to involve them in the design and development of systems are a necessity. And because computer-aided instruction is still largely experimental and varied in its methods and objectives, continued experimentation is wiser than fixing on one system now.

2. Library Systems and Subsystems

The needs that have brought computers into some library operations include the growing knowledge explosion as represented by printed works of all kinds, and the inability of library staffs to acquire, catalog, and eventually to house them in present library buildings. Computer-based information storage and retrieval systems were developed initially for various subsystems, such as for a particular professional journal, or for cataloging new acquisitions, or for use in specific subject-matter areas (particularly engineering and scientific fields). Some projects are under way to convert present card-catalog systems to computer-based ones.

Predictions about the fully computerized library of the future will be realized only many decades away, and even then there are likely to be many specialized and general book and periodical collections available for library readers and browsers. The experience with Project INTREX in the M.I.T. libraries suggests that this "experimental pilot model machine-stored library system" will grow and be useful to scholars interested in rapid information search and retrieval. Eventually the system will permit direct transfer of unpublished materials to the "on-line" intellectual community.

The implications of these possibilities for library staffs include the reduction of routine and time-consuming work, reorientation of staff functions to include assistance to users of the computer-based system, and enlargement of the other responsibilities of librarians. Library users will have the advantages of a man-machine interactive system in their literature search and systematic library-based research projects.

The interaction of computers, library staff, and users will require considerable care in implementation. Changes in present systems need the understanding and cooperation of staff people accustomed to long-existing ways of working with books and with users of library collections. Initial computer-based library information and retrieval systems will undoubtedly be modified many times to meet the needs of users, as well as to supplement effectively the nonprogrammable work of library staffs. Another future possibility is the conflict with present copyright laws

preventing reproduction of printed works without
publisher's or author's permission. As printed works are
stored, and reproduced in part by users at their request (as
is now happening with photocopying of printed materials),
the protection authors and publishers now have may be
substantially eroded.

3. Legal, Legislative and Related Services

Computer-based legal information storage and retrieval
systems have been growing because of expanding statutes,
court decisions, and administrative rulings. Low-paid law
clerks who might search law libraries are no longer
available, and law school graduates can be used more
effectively in other assignments. Some other computer-based
systems have been developed to help lawyers in drafting
wills, planning estates, handling trust administration, and
keeping office records. What has happened in many of
these is often experimental; the practice of law is still
probably less affected than the other knowledge-based
fields. The same is true of legislative services, where only a
few states have developed computer-based systems for
keeping track of the progress of bills through the
legislature.

In court administration, computers have been used in
scheduling cases and courtrooms, indexing cases, filing and
reproducing records, reproducing standard court forms, and
selecting jurors. But again, these applications are not
general, and resistances to changes in established ways of
doing things are great. Police departments seem to be less
resistant to uses of computers which speed apprehension of
criminals or wanted persons, or traffic violators who ignore
summonses. The increase in this information has swamped
some police departments, just as delays have plagued the
courts, so that computers that have been programmed to
record and transmit information quickly and accurately
have helped the humans involved to do their jobs more
effectively.

The implications of computer-based systems in these
related fields include the reduction in manual record
keeping, the speedier handling of increased information,

and the retrieval of machine-stored information. These developments will enable professionals and nonprofessional staffs in law offices, legislatures, courts, and police departments to cope with the vast quantities of information confronting them. It is unlikely that professionals will be displaced, but some clerical staffs attached to courts, for example, will probably not have to be expanded. Information may become more centralized, but if responsible professional people have access to the information base, they may improve the quality of their decisions in many separate locations: law offices, legislatures and legislative offices, courts, and police departments.

4. Medical and Hospital Services

The needs that brought computers to these services were similar to those in the other knowledge-based fields: the information explosion and the shortage of nonprofessional as well as professional personnel to deal with the expansion of records, lab reports, and medical knowledge generally. While initial efforts were to improve hospital record keeping and administration, computers have also been used in storing patients' records, preparing their medical histories prior to admission, and analyzing their electrocardiograms.

Recent largely experimental efforts have included computer-aided diagnosis for physicians, and other computer-based information and retrieval systems including patient scheduling, laboratory test reporting, and specialized medical information through medical libraries. It is likely that man-machine systems will spread in hospitals, clinics, and group medical practice more rapidly than in private medical practice. But private physicians who are not always able to keep abreast of the latest medical information, or who lack access to specialized hospital facilities for tests of various sorts, may find their professional capacities enlarged through computer-based systems.

Nonetheless, resistances will continue to preserve traditional methods of medical practice. While it is unlikely that professionals will soon be displaced because of persistent shortages, the practice of medicine and the organization and delivery of hospital services may well be changed more and more in the direction of man-machine systems. Where resistances retard this, systems designers will have to take more time to work with professionals and nonprofessionals alike, involving them in part of the design and implementation of the systems.

5. National and Centralized Local Data Banks
The need for comprehensive analysis of large bodies of economic and social data drawn from census, social security, and other demographic records has led to the proposal for a national data bank. Administrative requirements in counties and cities, on the other hand, account for the limited development of centralized local data banks. Thus the two needs and the two types of data banks are quite different.

Extensive panel reports and legislative hearings considered the national data bank proposal. Despite good reasons for such a data bank for research purposes and as an aid to national policy making, the issue of privacy of information on individuals in the system came to the fore in congressional hearings. This eventually resulted in the death of the proposal, at least in the immediate future. Proponents denied that individual data would ever be revealed; but some responsible critics pointed out that insufficient protection of individual privacy had been built into the proposed system. Other critics used scare tactics to defeat the proposal.

Strangely enough, the issue of individual privacy has seldom been raised about the centralized local data banks, which contain detailed information about citizens as an aid to planning, administration of services, law enforcement, and record keeping. It seems likely that such computer-based information and retrieval systems will spread, and the question of individual privacy will have to be faced. Centralization of information about citizens need not expose individuals if protective procedures are built into the design and administration of the systems. Nor is it likely that centralization of such information will lead to highly centralized administration of public services. Access to aggregate information analyzed for specific purposes may well improve the quality of local administration at all levels. The national data bank would have helped to answer some of the questions plaguing policy makers at the national level, whether in the executive branch or in the Congress. And it would certainly help to improve the quality of social science research as an aid to policy making.

Some General Implications in All Fields

Following this brief review of experience in each of the five knowledge-based fields, it is helpful to consider briefly the general implications of computers in all five fields. These implications are future-oriented, although in some cases, as we have seen earlier, the future is already here.

1. Busy Specialists and Professionals Will Be Relieved of Time-Consuming Repetitive Parts of Their Work

In computer-aided instruction, teachers should have fewer drill-type duties, and computers may be able to assist them in grading routine papers and examinations. Library staffs will have less manual cataloging to do; they can use computers to handle new acquisitions to library collections, search machine-based catalogs for new research in fields of interest to users, and generally assist users in a computer-based library.

Lawyers will be relieved of tedious searching of statutes and court cases, court clerks of manual reocrd keeping and copying, police of manual record keeping and searching for wanted persons. Hospital staffs will have more time for subprofessional and professional duties, as record keeping, laboratory test reporting, and other paper work is computer-based. If the national data center should become a reality, research workers will be spared the tedious task of trying to collect data for special analyses, now available only in many separate data banks or sources.

2. People in These Fields Will Be Provided with Computer-Based Programs in Solving Problems or Advancing Their Knowledge

In computer-aided instruction, students will be able to set their own pace in structured subjects, either slower than in the classroom until they understand the sequence of the subject, or faster than the average if they are brighter or more advanced. In the computer-based libraries of the future, similar to Project INTREX, scholars and research workers will have rapid access to specialized collections of scholarly work, not only at their own institutions but through distant collections linked to the system. The on-line scholarly community will be widened through the transfer of work in progress, for comment and revision. Lawyers will have the help of a more extensive and rapid search of legal sources, judges will benefit from improved scheduling of cases and better indexing of previous cases, legislators will be aided by computer retrieval of the status of bills in progress, and police departments will be more effective with rapid access to files on criminals and wanted persons.

Hospital personnel will be helped by more rapid and accurate reporting of medical records and tests, and individual physicians may find their capacities enlarged by systems for rapid retrieval of all kinds of medical information, as well as by specialized systems to aid their diagnosis of disease and illness. With a national data bank, research workers would have access to a vastly more significant body of aggregate social and economic data than now exists.

3. Computer-Based Systems May Help to Reduce Shortages of Specialists and Professional Personnel

Computer-aided instruction should enable teachers to spend more time with students on less-structured parts of different subjects, and to deal with their special problems as they encounter them in their learning process. Relieved of drill-type teaching, they may be able to handle larger classes. In libraries, the shortage of library staff people such as catalogers may be relieved by machine-based catalog

systems. Lawyers may have more time for counsel
with clients if computers speed case preparation, trust
administration, and other duties.

The time of legislative staffs will be saved by information
retrieval systems, judges will be able to work more
efficiently with better access to case files, and police will be
released for professional duties as computers take over
information retrieval gathering and retrieval functions.
Physicians in short supply will find their medical skills
enlarged by computerized information retrieval and
diagnostic systems. Nurses and other hospital personnel,
also in short supply, will have to spend less time on record
keeping and routine information transfer tasks, leaving
more time for professional duties.

4. Man-Machine Interaction Systems Will Spread in These Fields

Students, programs, and teachers may be linked in an on-
line interactive system in a time-shared computer. The
teacher will become a resource person, available to the
student who is having difficulty with a program or
problem in his terminal, and the teacher may be able to
reply through a central terminal. Generally, however, the
interactive system of student and computer will involve the
teacher in person in most student-teacher contacts. Lawyers
or their assistants will interact with a central computer in
searching legal sources, as will legislators and their staffs as
they check the data file for past and present legislation.
Court clerks will use computers for scheduling, record
keeping, indexing, and other administrative uses, and
judges will parallel lawyers in their use of computer-based
legal sources. Police or civilian specialists in police
headquarters can assist policemen in the field by rapidly
checking computer-based data files on criminals and
wanted persons.

Library staffs will assist users with on-line queries of
computerized catalogs, and help them retrieve for their
personal use certain references or passages of cataloged
items. Doctors and hospital staff will use computer-based
files of patients' medical records, medical histories,

laboratory test results, and other medical information. In diagnosis, physicians will be assisted by a sequential, interactive computer-based system. If the national data bank ever materializes, research workers may be able to retrieve subunits of aggregate data for analysis on the computer.

5. Organizations Will Become More Centralized in Some of Their Functions, but Decentralized Decision Making May Also Be Strengthened

National or regional systems of computer-aided instruction may be developed by specialists within the school system, or at universities, or in the learning corporations. Regional educational computer utilities may grow, leading to some standardization of instructional programs. But individual school systems may also have a wider choice among available programs, and teachers may be able to design their own curricula from computer-based and individualized programs.

Library systems involving several libraries regionally or nationally will be encouraged by the availability of computer-based catalogs through interactive terminals. But this may also enrich the resources available to individual scholars or research teams. Small law offices may give up trying to have their own law libraries as they depend on central computerized legal source files, or as they use the services of computer utilities for other routine legal services.

Large court systems may have access to a central computer facility, but smaller ones will not; nor will small police departments, unless computer utilities grow in this field. In any case, decision making by court personnel and judges will be strengthened, not taken over, by the computer. The same will be true of medical practice and any part of hospital services involving the use of professional or subprofessional personnel. Information storage, processing, and retrieval will be handled through a central system or utility; but the person using the data will still have to make the decision involving the patient. Presumably, with better data, the chances for error and for inadequate diagnosis are less likely, but the responsibility is still that of the human, not the machine. While a national or centralized local data bank represents centralization of information, the individual scholar or administrator using the system will achieve better individual research results or improved administrative decisions as a consequence of access to this centralized data bank.

6. **In Each of These Fields, Resistance to Changing Traditional Ways of Working and Traditional Handling of Information Will Continue Unless Systems Designers Find Ways of Explaining What They Are Trying to Do and Involving Those Affected in the Design and Implementation of Computer-Based Systems**

The introduction of computer-aided instruction on a wide scale will involve school boards or committees, school administrators and teachers. In the words of one observer, "marathon sessions" between systems and school personnel will be needed. The same is true of computer introductions in libraries, where both library staff and users will have to be consulted and involved in systems design. Fears have to be overcome, people have to be trained, and ideas sought as systems are introduced in legal and legislative services, court administration, and crime prevention or law enforcement.

Involvement of physicians in the development of a computerized medical history system was found to be highly related to their acceptance and use of the system. Similar experiences are reported in the development of laboratory test reporting systems, in other information gathering and retrieval systems, and especially in computer-aided diagnosis. Professionals in most fields tend to use computer-based systems when they come to view them as sources of help rather than as potential threats to their professionalism.

The experience with the proposed national data bank illustrates another resistance to be met and overcome. The understandable concern for privacy of information about individuals cannot be lightly dismissed. Sufficient technical and adminstrative procedures should be developed in an

effort to calm the fears of critics, so that the legitimate
needs of research and policy planners for access to large
bodies of aggregate (not individual) data can be realized.
The centralized local data banks that have so far avoided
the privacy battle may well have to consider similar
safeguards before this issue rises to plague them.

.   .   .   .   .

This chapter may appropriately end with the thought
mentioned in the Introduction. One may be pessimistic
about short-run possibilities in computer-based programs in
each of these fields, because of resistances, slowness in
overcoming technical problems in hardware and software,
and the gap between extravagant claims and actual
performance in some cases. But over the long pull, the
computer revolution will certainly affect the way in which
work is done and how people function in all knowledge-
based fields, as it has already in the management of
enterprises. Professionals and specialists will find their
capabilities enlarged, not threatened, by the computer, and
they will accept this fact better if they are brought into
the development of systems earlier rather than later.

As the American experience develops, it is something of a
warning signal as well as a beacon lighting the way for
similar uses of computers in knowledge-based fields in other
countries, developed as well as less developed in economic
terms.

Index